Bloom's

GUIDES

Sandra Cisneros's
The House on
Mango Street

The Adventures of Huckleberry Finn

All the Pretty Horses

Animal Farm

The Autobiography of Malcolm X

The Awakening

The Bell Jar

Beloved

Beowulf

Black Boy

The Bluest Eye

Brave New World

The Canterbury Tales

Catch-22

The Catcher in the Rye

The Chosen

The Crucible

Cry, the Beloved Country

Death of a Salesman

Fahrenheit 451

A Farewell to Arms

Frankenstein

The Glass Menagerie

The Grapes of Wrath

Great Expectations

The Great Gatsby

Hamlet

The Handmaid's Tale

Heart of Darkness

The House on Mango Street

I Know Why the Caged Bird Sings

The Iliad

Invisible Man

Jane Eyre

The Joy Luck Club

The Kite Runner

Lord of the Flies

Macbeth

Maggie: A Girl of the Streets

The Member of the Wedding

The Metamorphosis

Native Son

Night

1984

The Odyssey

Oedipus Rex

Of Mice and Men

One Hundred Years of Solitude

Pride and Prejudice

Ragtime

A Raisin in the Sun

The Red Badge of Courage

Romeo and Juliet

The Scarlet Letter

A Separate Peace

Slaughterhouse-Five

Snow Falling on Cedars

The Stranger

A Streetcar Named Desire

The Sun Also Rises

A Tale of Two Cities

Their Eyes Were Watching God

The Things They Carried

To Kill a Mockingbird

Uncle Tom's Cabin

The Waste Land

Wuthering Heights

Bloom's

GUIDES

Sandra Cisneros's
The House on Mango Street

Edited & with an Introduction
by Harold Bloom

BLOOM'S
LITERARY CRITICISM
An imprint of Infobase Publishing

Bloom's Literary Criticism

An imprint of Infobase Publishing

132 West 31st Street

New York NY 10001

Library of Congress Cataloging-in-Publication Data

Sandra Cisneros's The house on Mango Street / edited and with an introduction by Harold Bloom. — New ed.

   p. cm. — (Bloom's guides)

 Includes bibliographical references and index.

 ISBN 978-1-60413-812-2

 1. Cisneros, Sandra. House on Mango Street. 2. Chicago (Ill.)—In literature. 3. Girls in literature. 4. Mexican Americans in literature. 5. American literature—History and criticism. 6. Authors, American. I. Bloom, Harold. II. Title: House on Mango Street.

 PS3553.I78H63 2010

 813'.54—dc22   2010005023

Bloom's Literary Criticism books are available at special discounts when purchased in bulk quantities for businesses, associations, institutions, or sales promotions. Please call our Special Sales Department in New York at (212) 967–8800 or (800) 322–8755.

You can find Bloom's Literary Criticism on the World Wide Web at http://www.chelseahouse.com

Contributing editor: Portia Williams Weiskel

Cover designed by Takeshi Takahashi

Composition by IBT Global, Troy NY

Cover printed by IBT Global, Troy NY

Book printed and bound by IBT Global, Troy NY

Date printed: May 2010

Printed in the United States of America

10 9 8 7 6 5 4 3 2 1

This book is printed on acid-free paper.

All links and Web addresses were checked and verified to be correct at the time of publication. Because of the dynamic nature of the Web, some addresses and links may have changed since publication and may no longer be valid.

Contents

Introduction

Rereading *The House on Mango Street*, some years after first encountering this book by Sandra Cisneros, is not for me a literary experience. What matters about this series of linked narratives is social testimony, or the anguish of a young woman confronting the dilemmas of Mexican-American identity. To an outsider, these in turn seem founded upon the vexed issue of Mexican national identity. As background (one among many) to *The House on Mango Street*, I suggest that we turn to the greatest of Mexican writers, the poet-critic and Nobel Prize Winner, Octavio Paz (1914–1998). His *The Labyrinth of Solitude* (1950) remains a disturbing guide to what could be called the Mexican myth of Mexico.

Doubtless there are and will be rival attempts to define what might be called the genius of Mexico, and some Mexican feminists already denounce *The Labyrinth of Solitude* for implicitly taking the side of what it exposes and criticizes, the Mexican male myth that their women first betrayed them to, and with, the invading Spaniards. And yet I cannot see how Paz could have been clearer:

> In contrast to Guadalupe, who is the Virgin Mother, the *Chingada* is the violated Mother. Neither in her nor in the Virgin do we find traces of the darker attributes of the great goddesses: the lasciviousness of Amaterasu and Aphrodite, the cruelty of Artemis and Astarte, the sinister magic of Circe or the bloodlust of Kali. Both of them are passive figures. Guadalupe is pure receptivity, and the benefits she bestows are of the same order: she consoles, quiets, dries tears, calms passions. The *Chingada* is even more passive. Her passivity is abject: she does not resist violence, but is an inert heap of bones, blood and dust. Her taint is constitutional and resides, as we have

7

said earlier, in her sex. This passivity, open to the outside world, causes her to lose her identity: she is the *Chingada*. She loses her name; she is no one; she disappears into nothingness; she is Nothingness. And yet she is the cruel incarnation of the feminine condition.

If the *Chingada* is a representation of the violated Mother, it is appropriate to associate her with the Conquest, which was also a violation, not only in the historical sense but also in the very flesh of Indian women. The symbol of this violation is Doña Malinche, the mistress of Cortés. It is true that she gave herself voluntarily to the conquistador, but he forgot her as soon as her usefulness was over. Doña Marina [the name given to La Malinche by the Spaniards] becomes a figure representing the Indian women who were fascinated, violated or seduced by the Spaniards. As a small boy will not forgive his mother if she abandons him to search for his father, the Mexican people have not forgiven La Malinche for her betrayal. She embodies the open, the *chingado*, to our closed, stoic, impassive Indians. Cuauhtémoc and Doña Marina are thus two antagonistic and complementary figures. There is nothing surprising about our cult of the young emperor—"the only hero at the summit of art," an image of the sacrificed son—and there is also nothing surprising about the curse that weighs against La Malinche. This explains the success of the contemptuous adjective *malinchista* recently put into circulation by the newspapers to denounce all those who have been corrupted by foreign influences. The *malinchistas* are those who want Mexico to open itself to the outside world: the true sons of Malinche, who is the *Chingada* in person. Once again we see the opposition of the close and the open.

Since Paz was writing as a poet, he received all the misunderstandings that he risked: "an elegant insult against Mexican mothers." More accurately, as Paz remarked, *"The Labyrinth of Solitude* was an attempt to describe and understand certain myths; at the same time, insofar as it is a literary work, it has in turn become another myth."

Whether or not Cisneros agrees with Paz, I cannot know, but his melancholy observations help me to contexualize *The House on Mango Street*.

Biographical Sketch

Sandra Cisneros was born on December 20, 1954, in the suburbs of Chicago, Illinois. Her family, which included six brothers, moved frequently between Mexico City and Chicago. With her transient lifestyle, it was often difficult for Cisneros to make and keep friends; consequently she became introverted and shy. At a young age, Cisneros began observing people—taking notes on their actions and conversations in a spiral notebook that she carried with her, and later incorporating her observations into the poetry and short stories she wrote when she was in grade school.

Cisneros read widely and wrote throughout her adolescence, though her inhibitions kept her from academic success as she was too shy to speak up in class. In the tenth grade, however, one of her teachers encouraged her to read some of her stories to the class. Cisneros received positive feedback from the class and gained confidence. She began working on the school's literary magazine and eventually became its editor. Henceforth, Cisneros became "the poet" to her classmates.

Cisneros continued her education at Loyola University in Chicago, and in 1976 she earned a B.A. in English. In the late 1970s, Cisneros's talent gained her admittance to the famed University of Iowa Writers' Workshop. The workshop proved to be a turning point for her as she engaged and developed her voice. It was during these workshops that she realized her own experiences were quite different from the rest of the students in the class as well as from the majority of Americans. From that point on, Cisneros decided to incorporate her experiences as an underprivileged bicultural Chicana female growing up in the United States into her writing. To this day, Cisneros relies heavily on her own memories when developing storylines for her strong, independent, female characters. Her "awakening" experience in the writers' workshop eventually led her to write *The House on Mango Street*, which was published by Arte Publico Press in 1984 and won the Before Columbus Foundation's American Book Award in 1985.

After obtaining her master's degree, Cisneros spent three years teaching at Latino Youth Alternative High School in Chicago. In the 1980s Cisneros earned a variety of fellowships and guest lectureships including two from the National Endowment for the Arts, one for fiction (1982) and one for poetry (1987). During this time, she wrote a collection of poetry titled *My Wicked, Wicked Ways* (1987). Susan Bergholz, her literary agent, encouraged her to publish a collection of short stories, and *Woman Hollering Creek* appeared in 1991 to wide acclaim. The collection won the PEN Center West Award for Best Fiction of 1991, the Quality Paperback Book Club New Voices Award, the Anisfield-Wolf Book Award, the Lannan Foundation Literary Award, and was selected as a notable book of the year by *The New York Times* and the *American Library Journal*. In 1995, Cisneros won the prestigious MacArthur Foundation Fellowship.

Sandra Cisneros's body of work includes three volumes of fiction, *Caramelo* (2002), *The House on Mango Street* (1983) and *Woman Hollering Creek and Other Stories* (1991), and four volumes of poetry, *Bad Boys* (1980), *The Rodrigo Poems* (1985), *My Wicked, Wicked Ways* (1987), and *Loose Woman* (1994). She is also the author of a bilingual children's book, *Hairs/Pelitos* (1994).

The Story Behind the Story

As a young girl growing up in multiple urban spaces, Sandra Cisneros endured many of the same growing pains as her protagonist, Esperanza, though the more removed she became from her upbringing the further she found herself distanced from the material that would serve as the basis of her best work. Government aid enabled her to attend college, and while there, a writer-in-residence encouraged her to attend graduate school. On that recommendation, Cisneros applied and was accepted into the Iowa Writers' Workshop, the most prestigious graduate writing program in the country. In an interview with Martha Satz given in 1985, Cisneros said "It was a bit of a shock to be in a program like the one at Iowa. It's a disciplined and rigorous program. I think I entered there a different person from the one who left." During her first year in the program, Cisneros found she was so intimidated that she wrote nearly nothing. She was the only person of Latino descent, much less Chicana, and her background of urban, multiethnic living set her apart from the other students.

In a now infamous class, Cisneros and her fellow students were discussing Gaston Bachelard's *Poetics of Space* wherein her professor referred to the "house of memory" as a comforting conceptual space. Cisneros vociferously contested the notion, believing that this concept could only be thought comforting by a man who had neither cleaned nor cared for a house. She knew her point of view was different, that she viewed words like *home* and *memory* with an uneasiness that none of her fellow students shared. Home had long been a word for ramshackle houses that embarrassed her, and her memory was filled with a host of diverse characters from the streets of the barrio. In retrospect, Cisneros commented, "I think it was important for me to have the culture shock I experienced at Iowa, for me to experience my otherness, in order for me to choose my subject intentionally." Ultimately it forced her to consider what she could write about that no one else could. That something was the barrio, and Cisneros began to write about her experiences there.

After graduating with an M.A. from the University of Iowa in 1978, Cisneros went to work at Latino Youth Alternative High School in Chicago. In many respects, the job returned her to her childhood roots. Though the students drained her emotionally, they also provided her with more stories to add to her own memories of coming of age in the city. After that stint, she worked at Loyola University of Chicago as an administrative assistant and counselor to minority and disadvantaged students. When she saw their hopeless situations, she vowed to "give back" in some way. Armed with her own stories and devoted to telling the stories of her mother, her aunt, and the other Chicana women and disenfranchised people around her, Cisneros began writing *The House on Mango Street*.

She claims that the work emerged from her desire to add perspective to the barrio stories told by men. In her interview with Martha Satz, she recalled:

> I have lived in the barrio, but I discovered later on in looking at works by my contemporaries that they write about the barrio as a colorful, Sesame Street-like, funky neighborhood. To me the barrio was a repressive community. I found it frightening and very terrifying for a woman. The future for women in the barrio is not a wonderful one. You don't wander around these "mean streets." You stay at home. If you do have to get somewhere, you take your life in your hands. So I wanted to counter those colorful viewpoints, which I'm sure are true to an extent but were not true for me.

Her fresh perspective intrigued both critics and readers.

When the book first appeared in print, critics were generally positive about the authentic voice, the attention to detail, the music of the language, and the sheer impact of the coming-of-age story. Cisneros was awarded the Before Columbus American Book Award in 1985. Still, some critics took exception to her portrayal of men, claiming that it was too generalized, portraying them all as predatory and dangerous. Others claimed that the book was particularly insulting to

Chicano men and destructive to their already compromised, often overtly biased portrayal in the mass media. Still others objected to Cisneros's refusal to align her work with a specific genre, thereby forcing critics to re-evaluate the way in which they judge her writing. The book is part prose poetry, part novel, and part young girl's diary. Despite its critics, Cisneros and her book have enjoyed much success. The fact that it is read in high school and college courses and enjoys a popular following attests to its wide appeal. Although the book was originally published by a small press, Arte Publico, Random House eventually opted to acquire the publishing rights. The move, six years after its initial publication, from a small press to a worldwide publishing conglomerate, suggests that *The House on Mango Street* has earned its place among the best contemporary coming-of-age novels.

List of Characters

Esperanza Cordero is the adolescent protagonist who tells her coming-of-age story through vignettes relating her sensory impressions of the world around her and the actual events of her life. She dreams throughout the narrative for a house of her own which she eventually realizes will be achieved through writing.

Nenny is Esperanza's little sister. Throughout the novel, Esperanza feels increasingly separated from her younger sister, due to her own maturation. Her sister is also the only person with whom Esperanza shares an intimate understanding of what it means to live in Mexico, thereby reinforcing her close ties to family.

Mama is an accomplished and talented woman who chooses to leave school because she does not consider her clothes nice enough to wear in public. As a result of her regret, she urges Esperanza to embrace education and learn all she can so that she will not be dependent or feel trapped.

Papa is a gardener for the wealthy. Esperanza often defines him by what he allows and does not allow her to do.

Carlos and **Kiki** are Esperanza's brothers. They communicate with their sisters inside the house, but outside they ignore them, maintaining the gender power divisions of the neighborhood.

Cathy is a neighborhood girl who befriends Esperanza for a week before her family moves to a more affluent neighborhood. Her brief presence in the story reinforces the transient nature of the barrio and the socioeconomic stratification between the various ethnic groups.

Lucy and **Rachel** are girls from Texas who befriend Esperanza and with whom she buys a share in a bike. With them,

Esperanza comes of age, reinforcing the idea that for Chicanas the experience of acculturation is communal.

Meme Ortiz is a boy who moves into Cathy's old house and with whom Esperanza has a jumping contest. Meme's desire to prove himself in the new neighborhood overwhelms his common sense as he breaks both of his arms trying to win the contest. His broken arms suggest that few can escape the barrio.

Marin is Esperanza's cousin who lives in the Ortiz's basement apartment. She emerges as one representative of the Chicana female—beautiful but stuck in the house babysitting. Her sexual power is muted by the men of her family; nonetheless it is also the only means by which she might escape her current life. She must barter her body for marriage in order to escape the barrio. Through her, Esperanza gains greater awareness of the ways in which her gender can empower or imprison her.

Louie's cousin, though never given a specific name, is important because he returns to the neighborhood in a Cadillac convertible to show what he has accomplished. Sadly, the accomplishment is illusive, but it strengthens Esperanza's resolve to return to her community with work of real merit.

Rose Vargas is a woman with too many ill-behaved children. She is another victim of the patriarchal system in Chicano culture. Because Rose's husband has left her to care for so many children alone, everyone in the community, including Rose and her children, see her problem as being too big to remedy and thereby cease to care about the welfare of the Vargas children.

Alicia is an older girl in the neighborhood who attends college as a way to escape her life as surrogate mother and wife after the death of her mother. She provides a positive role model for Esperanza as she has found a way out of the barrio through education.

Darius is a bully who picks on girls and skips school. He does, however, say something profound that Esperanza will remember for the rest of her life. He points at the clouds and tells Esperanza, "That's God." Esperanza is moved by this simple expression of faith.

Aunt Lupe is Esperanza's aunt, a woman who was formerly an accomplished swimmer. Sadly, Lupe has been stricken by an illness that eventually kills her. She urges Esperanza to never stop writing.

Elenita is the woman who tells fortunes and predicts that Esperanza will have a house of her own, "a home in the heart." Her prediction is important because Esperanza begins to think of home as something created on the interior, as a collection of stories.

Geraldo is the young man who is killed by a hit-and-run accident while Marin is with him. For Esperanza, Geraldo becomes a symbol of the way in which identity is lost between Mexico and the United States. He belongs to no country, and no one claims him when he dies.

Ruthie lives with her mother, Edna, who owns the large building next door to Esperanza. She comes to live with her mother after her marriage fails. It is unclear whether marriage caused her childlike mental state or whether her mental state caused the dissolution of the marriage. Ruthie claims that she used to write children's books. Esperanza befriends her, showing her compassion and commitment to the disenfranchised.

Sire is a neighborhood boy who has romantic feelings for the maturing Esperanza.

Mamacita is the large, beautiful, Mexican woman who moves into the neighborhood. She is bereft at having to leave her country, and Esperanza empathizes with her feelings of dislocation and her powerlessness in controlling what happens to her.

Rafaela is a young woman married to a man who keeps her locked in the house. She leans out her window dreaming of another life and becomes for Esperanza an example of how some men imprison women to control and suppress their sexual power.

Sally is a young woman about Esperanza's age whose father beats her and imprisons her in his home.

Minerva is a young woman, only a little older than the adolescent Esperanza, who has two children and a husband who beats her. Minerva and Esperanza share their poetry with each other. She serves a cautionary function in the book, reinforcing the idea that sometimes marriage is not an escape but a potential prison.

The Three Sisters are elderly aunts of Lucy and Rachel. They tell Esperanza that she will escape from the barrio but that she must return for the others who cannot leave.

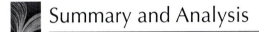

Summary and Analysis

Before entering the text, readers receive insight into Cisneros's project with her dedication, "A las Mujeres to the Women." She dedicates her book in both English and Spanish, reinforcing her own dual ethnic background, to the women in her life. In doing so, she also acknowledges that a large part of her struggle for identity in the barrio was driven by issues of gender.

Cisneros chooses to tell the story in a series of vignettes that occupy their own liminal space. The stories resist assignation to a particular form, floating comfortably between prose poetry, the novel, and journal writing. In many ways, resistance forms the core of the book. Cisneros's *The House on Mango Street* resists form, gender stereotypes, cultural norms, and prefabricated futures for the characters it portrays.

Cisneros chooses to use the voice of a child in the throes of puberty to tell her story. This is a savvy choice, allowing Esperanza to observe without passing judgment. Readers, therefore, bring their own cultural associations to the significant details Esperanza presents. Cisneros keeps her authorial intrusion minimal in adopting the girl's voice, thereby resisting the urge to be overtly political.

The book opens with a chapter of the same name, setting the scene early and offering information that contextualizes the house and its significance to the family. Esperanza, the protagonist, a girl on the brink of puberty explains, "We didn't always live on Mango Street." What she remembers from her early childhood is moving from one place to another as the family grew larger and needed more space. Eventually, they find the house on Mango Street, and although the children have more freedom there to make noise and play without the interference of other children from the apartment building, it still does not fulfill Esperanza's (or her family's) expectations for a first house. Her parents have little choice in what they buy due to a meager budget and a compelling impetus to move. The house on Mango Street represents the best of the Cordero family's options, but for Esperanza, whose dreams were based on the houses she saw on television, her small ramshackle residence with its one bedroom for an entire family of six is shameful and depressing. Critic Julian Olivarez claims "Mango Street is a street sign, a marker, that circumscribes the neighborhood to its Latino population of Puerto Ricans, Chicanos, and Mexican immigrants. This house is not the protagonist's dream house; it is only a temporary house" (235). Esperanza recalls feeling ashamed from an incident in the past when a nun asked her to point her home out in their former neighberhood on Loomis Street. The nun's disgusted and incredulous tone when Esperanza points to the dilapidated third floor of a house shames the child. The nun's assumption is clearly based on ethnic stereotypes, and though Esperanza does not acknowledge this, the woman's comments and incredulity make Esperanza "feel like nothing." The first chapter ends with Esperanza's fervent statement of her quest: "I knew then that I had to have a house. A real house. One I could point to." The "sad red house" is not the sort of home to be proud of, not like the ones on television, and though her parents keep saying that the house is a temporary solution, she does not believe them. Esperanza realizes that her family will never be able to provide more than the temporary houses in which they have been living. This reinforces her desire and drive to eventually own a respectable home of her own.

Within this first chapter, Esperanza immediately indicates the gap between the white middle-class families portrayed on television and the Latino experience in the barrio of Chicago. The white world has three bathrooms to the Cordero's one and enough bedrooms for every child to have his or her own. Esperanza also recognizes that, in order to participate in the broader white American world, she needs to inhabit a house that is a visible manifestation of success and assimilation. For her, the home is a way to assume a public persona and eventually a place wherein she might assume an identity for her community. Her identity becomes inextricably interconnected with her home environment. Leslie Gutiérrez-Jones articulates Esperanza's desire:

Acutely aware of the disempowerment that results from lacking "a home of one's own," she yearns to stake out an architectural space—one which she implicitly assumes will provide her with the "space" to develop a sense of identity and an artistic voice. However, when architecture will not cooperate, she must look instead to her imagination in order to create a sense of space—one which can, in turn, provide a place for her writing. (296)

In the next chapter, **"Hair,"** Esperanza provides the reader with a strong sense of her domesticated mother. The girl associates the smell of bread with her mother's hair. She speaks of the pin curls her mother makes in an effort to look pretty and the way her mother moves over to make room in the bed for her children while her Papa sleeps blissfully through the commotion. Esperanza remembers the sounds of rain and her father's snoring as her mother holds her. Within this description, the mother belongs exclusively to the family and the household she runs. It is Mama who makes room in the bed when a child is scared and Papa who remains asleep and unaware of the goings on around him. Throughout the vignette, Esperanza's depictions re-create a sense of comfort and belonging, subtly reinforcing the strength of her family ties.

In the chapter titled **"Boys & Girls,"** Esperanza continues her observations in regard to gender and family. She points out that in the Cordero home her siblings all speak to one another, but outside it, the boys have their own lives and never interact with the girls. This segregation mimics the lives of the older people in the community and reinforces the gender stratifications that exist outside marriage. Without her brothers, Esperanza is left with her younger sister, Nenny. Nenny is too young to be the friend that Esperanza wants, one to whom she will not have to explain jokes, one to whom she can tell her secrets. The short chapter ends with Esperanza dreaming of being a red balloon, "a balloon tied to an anchor." Clearly, the balloon is a metaphor for escape, one of many throughout the book, but equally clear is the pull of her familial duties. An anchor tied to the balloon keeps it earthbound and stationary, representing Nenny's association to Esperanza in the story.

Esperanza's observations of cultural disparity continue as she critically examines her name in **"My Name."** In the United States, it means hope; in Meixco, it means sorrow. To Esperanza, it means bad luck, ill fate, and the sounds of her father's Mexican records. She associates grief and bad luck with her Spanish name due to her namesake, her great-grandmother, who like her descendant was born "in the Chinese year of the horse—which is supposed to be bad luck if you're born female." Esperanza does not believe this, insisting it is yet another story meant to keep women oppressed and powerless. She says, "I think this is a Chinese lie, because the Chinese, like the Mexicans, don't like their woman strong." This observation pinpoints Esperanza's awareness of what kind of life the women lead within her community. She resists the idea of women being powerless, preferring instead the legends of her wild grandmother who refused to marry. Esperanza explains further how her willful grandmother was abducted and forced to marry. She tells the reader how her grandmother was carried off "as if she were a fancy chandelier."

This story teaches Esperanza that to be a woman is to be a commodity, one that can be bought, sold, and even stolen. She continues the story, claiming that her grandmother never forgave her grandfather; instead she spent the rest of her life looking out a window, "the way so many women sit their sadness on an elbow." This image of women staring out windows pining for some sort of freedom or independence from their husbands or fathers is one that returns throughout the book. For Esperanza, it figures as a prison with a princess hidden away never to come out. In her world, princes do not rescue but imprison the princess. As she continues to think about her name, she begins to wish for a name more like a superhero or a mythic woman, giving in to her dream of escape. Critic Tomoko Kuribayashi claims that "Cisneros' narrative highlights how language—and taking control of it—is a determining factor for Esperanza's future. Taking control of language is taking control of one's spatial experiences" (169). In a way, it means writing oneself out of one's current course and destiny. Critic Julian Olivarez sees Esperanza's renaming as a way of denying the patriarchy: "Esperanza prefers a name not culturally embedded in a dominating, male-centered ideology" (236).

"Cathy, Queen of Cats" is both the title of the next chapter and the girl who offers Esperanza advice on who to associate with in their neighborhood, basing her suggestions on societal prejudices. Cathy tells her to stay away from a man she calls "the baby-grabber," two "raggedy" girls, and a woman who became stuck up after college. There is also a woman who used to own an apartment building and begged her son not to sell it. The son agreed but then sold the building anyway. Cathy figures men as evil, selling things out from under women, preying on innocents, reinforcing Esperanza's idea that men are dangerous and oppressive. After observing Esperanza, Cathy agrees to be her friend but only for a week. Her family is moving to a better neighborhood, because she says "the neighborhood is getting bad." Even though Esperanza is young, she is wise enough to realize two things about Cathy and her family. One, Cathy is simply repeating what she hears her parents say, and two, Cathy's parents are moving because of the influx of Chicano families like Esperanza's.

Esperanza eventually has a good day in her new neighborhood. While walking with Cathy, her temporary friend, Esperanza meets Rachel and Lucy, rag-tag sisters from Texas, who want five dollars for their friendship so they can buy a new bike. Esperanza, desperate for friends and some sign that she fits in, takes three of her own dollars and two of her unknowing sister's and invests in the bike, losing snobbish Cathy in the process but acquiring two nonjudgmental friends and a mode of escape, the bike. The three girls agree to take turns, each owning the bike once every three days. The ownership of the bike speaks to the circumstances of the barrio. To own something often requires the aid of others, as few people can afford to buy things on their own. It also speaks to the communal attitude that marks Esperanza's later comments in regard to her house and her faith in writing. She intends to help others get out of their own particular situations.

In the next chapter, Esperanza turns her attention to her sister, Nenny, remarking that they look nothing alike at first glance, not like her new friends Lucy and Rachel whose facial features clearly indicate they are related. Instead, the bond between Nenny and Esperanza is revealed in their mannerisms and in their shared experiences, acquired from years of living together. When Esperanza comments, "Look at that house . . . it looks like Mexico," she is comforted by the fact that her sister understands. Nenny is one of the few people with whom Esperanza shares the same cultural literacy. This literacy, in some ways, exiles Esperanza from the people around her, but at the same time it strengthens her familial ties.

In **"Gil's Furniture Bought & Sold,"** Esperanza ventures into the local junk store where everything is piled precariously. The store is a maze in which a child might get lost. At the center of Gil's is the old man who owns the shop. During one visit with her sister, Nenny finds an old music box and asks the owner about it. He winds the victrola, and sound pours out, entrancing both Esperanza and Nenny. A moment later, Esperanza, catching herself becoming interested, turns away, pretending that she does not care. She thinks her sister is stupid for caring and asking how much it costs. In this "are you tough enough" neighborhood, to show too much love for beauty is childish and dangerous, an admission of immaturity and weakness.

In the next vignette, Esperanza describes her new neighbor, a young man who calls himself Meme, though his name is Juan. He lives in Cathy, the Queen of Cats' former house, built by Cathy's father with slanted floors and crooked stairs. It is in Meme's backyard that he and the neighborhood kids host the "First Annual Tarzan Jumping Contest." Meme wins but in the process breaks both of his arms. Winning is important to the children, and Meme willingly accepts the consequences. He has proved himself in the neighborhood and feels good about it.

Downstairs from the Ortiz's, in the rented basement apartment, live Louie's family, from Puerto Rico. His cousin Marin lives with them, and though she wears make-up and nylons and claims to be in love, her nearest contact with the outside world is in the doorway of her home. She is forced into babysitting her young relatives because she is a woman, an early example of the imprisoned women that Esperanza observes throughout the book. Louie's other cousin drives into the neighborhood one afternoon in a yellow Cadillac convertible. All of the children clamor for rides, asking the man where he got the car. He takes them for a ride around the neighborhood but never answers the question. Intoxicated with the power windows and luxury of the Cadillac, the children press buttons and play with controls. By the seventh time around the block, police sirens are sounding. Louie's cousin orders all of the children out of the car and speeds off. The chase ends with the car crashing into a tree and the young man in handcuffs. His return to the neighborhood speaks to Esperanza's dream of leaving the barrio and returning a success. This young man comes back to his neighborhood to show what he has achieved (even if by criminal means). Sadly, he also gives the impression that one of the few ways out of the barrio is through crime.

Marin becomes the focal point of the next chapter, **"Marin."** Unlike Esperanza and her friends, Marin wears make-up and understands boys. She dreams of working downtown in a job where she can wear nice clothes and be seen by men, with the hope that one might marry her and take her away to his home in the suburbs. Every night she stands on the front porch after her mother goes to sleep and waits for the boys to pass by and look at her. Esperanza, in her careful study of Marin as a female archetype, realizes that Marin has pinned all of her hopes of escape on men. Marriage is Marin's chosen escape from the barrio. The critic Olivarez sees this as a continuation of the "dialect of inside/outside, of confinement and desire for the freedom of the outside world . . ." (234).

Esperanza directly addresses race and ethnicity and their relation to inclusion and exclusion in **"Those Who Don't."** She watches people come into her neighborhood, scared that they will be attacked. Here, "All brown all around," there is no difference to fear. She knows every strange figure in the neighborhood. Even when Louie's cousin returns with his stolen car, the children greet him as a friend, because of his relation to the neighborhood. With knowledge comes lack of fear and, with that, a kind of power. Still, she recognizes that white people are not the sole perpetuators of racial distrust. She notes that her family also rolls the windows up tight in a neighborhood "of another color." She muses that this is "how it goes and goes."

In the next chapter, Esperanza introduces Rose Vargas and her brood of ill-behaved children. Because there are so many and they behave so badly, the entire community, including the children and Rose, becomes indifferent to the well-being of these children. As a result, no one notices when Angel Vargas, a small child, climbs to the top of roof and throws herself off. Esperanza outlines the apathy created when people are overwhelmed.

In **"Alicia Who Sees Mice,"** Esperanza again comments on the fate of women in her culture. Alicia is a young woman in the neighborhood who attends college, believing that education might be her means out of the neighborhood. She is also a surrogate mother to her siblings and a surrogate housekeeper for her father. She has inherited her "mama's rolling pin and sleepiness" and wakes early to make tortillas. Olivarez notes that "Here we do not see the tortilla as a symbol of cultural identity but as a symbol of a subjugating ideology, of sexual domination, of the imposition of a role that the young woman must assume" (237). This young woman goes to bed so exhausted she hallucinates mice that keep her up at night. Her father orders her to sleep so she can again wake early and provide for her siblings before taking two trains and a bus to college, which might prove to be her salvation from marriage or life in a factory.

In the next chapter, Esperanza introduces Darius, who bullies little girls and skips school. Esperanza talks about the sky being one of the few beautiful things that exist in the barrio. This thought reminds her of Darius and a profound thing he once said to her. He had been looking at the sky and then pointed to the clouds telling her, "That's God." Esperanza marvels at how simple and true the observation is. The sky is one of the beautiful things that make it into the barrio, and it cannot be taken away by poverty or prejudice.

The topic of clouds comes up again in **"And Some More."** Esperanza, Nenny, Rachel, and Lucy begin to talk about the number of different Inuit names for snow. In the next lines, they bicker about the type of snow and the number of names a cousin has, at least one for each identity (American and Spanish), before discussing the different names of clouds. As they identify the different types of clouds, names from the neighborhood are being repeated, all the different types of people who live in the barrio, all the different types of Spanish names. The girls get into an argument over a description of a cloud that includes a reference to a face. They try to outtalk one another, exchanging insults and eventually creating a cacophony of voices. The chapter ends with the girls realizing that their argument is stupid and not worth risking their friendship over. Critic Leslie Gutiérrez-Jones believes that the competing voices symbolize Cisneros's emphasis on communal and collective identity making. Gutiérrez-Jones writes:

> The competing voices eventually blend to produce a sort of harmony—even a wry simple wisdom—in a way that monologic narrative would not allow. Such rhetorical instances mark yet another aspect of Esperanza's unique development toward an artistic voice and a sense of self which achieves an ongoing balance between connection and separation (309).

In **"The Family of Little Feet,"** the girls have another collective experience when they receive a bag of shoes from a family in the neighborhood. The multicolored shoes are exciting to the girls, offering them the chance to pretend to be Cinderella, or an older girl who attracts men like flies. As they swap shoes and try them on, Lucy orders them to take their socks off, and when they do they realize that they have legs like the older girls, the kind that potentially draw the attention of men. They walk down the street to the grocery store. Around them, the men are abuzz, some indignant and wanting to protect the girls from growing up too quickly, others filled with lascivious intent. The grocer tells the girls to take the high heels off claiming, "Them are dangerous," and a boy on a bicycle cries out "Ladies, lead me to heaven." So unaccustomed are they to being viewed as adults it takes the girls a few moments to realize that he is speaking to them. Critic Michelle Scalise Sugiyama writes:

> Their resolution to never go back to wearing the other kind of shoes comes after they realize that the shoes make them sexually attractive to men. . . . This power to arouse men and to make women jealous initially exhilarates them—they "just keep strutting," enjoying for the moment their position as the source of power rather than the object (10).

As they pass the laundromat, they make some of the other women jealous of the shoes they have. Their sense of empowerment dies, however, when they meet a homeless man who compliments them and offers a dollar for a kiss. Suddenly, the male attention that brought so much pleasure is now rife with potential violence. The girls run from him and decide they are tired of being beautiful. For the first time, they encounter the hungry gaze of the male sexual predator, and the experience so frightens them that when Lucy's mother throws the shoes out a few days later, none of the girls utters a whisper of complaint.

"A Rice Sandwich" chronicles another epiphany for Esperanza. Everyday she goes home for lunch, envying the children who remain at school to eat in the cafeteria. The cafeteria or "canteen" as she calls it, becomes a fixation for Esperanza; she wants to know what goes on there and convinces her mother to write a note to school explaining that Esperanza is too weak to walk to and from school in the middle of the day. The nun allows her to stay at school for one day, so Esperanza gets her wish; she goes to the canteen but only after meeting with Mother Superior who questions her until Esperanza is in tears. In her office, the nun, unwilling to grant the girl's request, asks Esperanza to point her house out, saying, "'You don't live far,' she says . . . 'I bet I can see your house from my window. Which one?' she said pointing to a row of ugly 3-flats, the ones even the raggedy men are ashamed to go to. Yes, I nodded even though I knew that wasn't my house and began to cry." The experience reveals for Esperanza the nun's beliefs concerning the possibilities for Mexican families. Critic Ellen McCracken believes that this strengthens Esperanza's resolve:

> It is in response to humiliations such as these that the autobiographical protagonist expresses a need for a house of her own. Rather than mere desire to possess private property, Esperanza's wish for a house represents a positive objectification of the self, the chance to redress humiliation and establish a dignified sense of her own personhood (65).

When she finally enters the cafeteria, she is crying, her lunch is soggy, and all of the other children are watching her. After all of her persuasive rhetoric, Esperanza finds she no longer wants to be in this hostile environment that turns out to be nothing very interesting at all. Again, she is forced to recognize the boundaries of inclusion and exclusion.

In **"Chanclas,"** Esperanza shops with her mother for a new dress to wear to her cousin's baptism. Her mother buys her a new dress, slip, and socks. By the end of the trip, her mother is too tired to buy Esperanza new shoes, and they leave without them. While her mother is shopping, Esperanza waits by the door, allowing no one in except her mother, another small reality of her life. She dresses for the party and puts on her old shoes, feeling sure that they have overshadowed the effect of the rest of her newly bought items. Again, Esperanza returns to the eroticism of the feet. When she arrives at the party, she sits in a chair, tucking her feet beneath the seat in an effort to hide them. When she is asked to dance by a boy, she refuses, afraid to show her shoes. Her Uncle Nacho then asks her to dance and drags the unwilling Esperanza to the floor. Her body follows her uncle's lead, remembering all that it was taught about dancing, and the two are complimented by the people watching. With all of the compliments and fanfare, Esperanza eventually forgets that her shoes are old and serviceable, bought because they last. Instead, all she hears is the clapping of the crowd as the music stops. When she returns to her seat, her mother is proud. Throughout the rest of the night, the boy who asked her to dance, who she suddenly sees as a man, watches her. She is excited by the idea of being wanted by this man. Scalise Sugiyama notes that:

> Esperanza's self-esteem is dependent upon the arousing male interest. . . . The male definition of beauty, exemplified by high heels, is psychologically as well as physically crippling as it requires, ultimately, submission and dependence. Compliance with this beauty standard is one of the ways in which, as Maria Herrara-Sobek puts it, "women are socialized into being participants in their own oppression" (18).

Esperanza is becoming increasingly aware of her sexuality and the powers and limits that accompany it. This becomes particularly apparent in the next chapter.

"Hips" is a pivotal chapter because Esperanza emphatically articulates the chasm caused by age and knowledge between herself and her sister, Nenny. The chapter begins with Lucy, Rachel, Esperanza, and Nenny skipping rope, talking about hips. Rachel claims, "They're good for holding a baby while you're cooking." Esperanza immediately feels disgusted. Rachel cannot move outside the realm of her own knowledge and experience to imagine something different, beyond gender roles. Lucy suggests hips are needed to dance. Nenny claims that, without them, one becomes a boy. Esperanza counters all arguments with science, a seemingly infallible discipline, and an insight she has derived from the college student, Alicia. Hips widen to allow mothers to give birth to their children. Beyond science though, Esperanza wants to discuss a broader, more imminent question: Do they want hips? Will they know what to do with them once they get them? The questions reflect her insecurities about taking on both the body and the roles of a woman. Esperanza describes a woman's walk as "if half of you wanted to go one way and the other half the other" (50). Nenny answers naively that the walk is meant to rock babies. Esperanza immediately wants to discount her younger sibling, but after thinking about it she realizes that this idea may not be so far-fetched and that her sister may not be so distant from her after all. Lucy starts to dance, claiming that "you gotta get the rhythm," and the girls begin to concoct rhymes that match the rhythm of the dances. While the older girls are chanting their new rhymes, Nenny continues to recite the old ones she already knows. Esperanza's fierce protection of her sister keeps the other girls from saying anything, but it does not keep Esperanza from thinking once again that her sister is still a child and that she, Esperanza, and their friends, Lucy and Rachel, have transcended that stage of their life. As Olivarez puts it:

> Suddenly the awareness of time passing and of growing up is given a spatial dimension. Esperanza, on the outside, is looking at Nenny inside the arc of the swinging rope that now separates Nenny's childhood dimension from her present awareness of just having left behind that very same childhood (238).

The girls, excluding Nenny, are now well on their way into puberty and with that comes the acquisition of a certain set of culturally derived expectations based on gender and socioeconomic status.

One such expectation shown in the next chapter, **"The First Job,"** is that the children in the family will get jobs to help their parents pay for the Catholic school they attend. For the Cordero family, there is no question of going to public school. Her father forbids it because "nobody goes to public school unless you wanted to turn out bad." His judgment is twofold. First, he believes that a Catholic education will lead to spiritual success, particularly in light of the fact that it reinforces gender roles in the family, but also because inner-city public schools are notoriously poorly financed and maintained. In an effort to get a job quickly, Esperanza has already gotten her social security number and imagines herself working at a typical job in a dime store or a hot dog stand. When Esperanza comes home from school one day, her mother and her aunt are waiting for her with a job plan. She is to work at the Peter Pan Photo Finishers where her aunt is employed. They coach Esperanza to claim she is a year older than she actually is in order to begin working without the interference of child labor laws. The next morning, Esperanza puts on a navy dress that makes her look older than her years and borrows money for lunch and her fare, knowing that she has a full week before she gets paid from her new job. For the interview, she lies about her age and gets the job. At work, she wears gloves and matches photos with their negatives. The hours are long, and she grows tired but is too shy to ask if she can sit. She mimics the behavior of the women beside her, gratefully sitting when they do. Her shyness backfires when the two women figure out what she is doing and laugh at her, finally telling her that she can sit down whenever she wants to. To hide her embarrassment, she relies on bravado, claiming that she already knew that, but their laughter only exacerbates her feelings of exclusion.

Her shyness continues to make the job difficult. When she is too scared to go into a lunchroom of strangers and eat, she hides in the washroom, eating her lunch and resuming her work early. When the next break comes, she hides in the cloak room, watching people punch in for the next shift. While she sits there, an older Asian man sits down to talk to her. Esperanza is happy to have the company until the man claims it is his birthday and asks for a kiss. She figures that there is no harm in kissing an old man for his birthday, but when she moves to kiss his cheek, he grabs her face and forces a kiss onto her mouth. The older she becomes, the more Esperanza develops a need, born of experience, to view men as dangerous predators. This continued pattern of abuse, harassment, and potential harm upsets some critics as they say it is an unfair portrayal of men and Chicano men in particular.

Still, in contrast to that point of view, in the next chapter, Esperanza is awakened by her father. He tells her, in his native Spanish, that her grandmother is dead and then he begins to cry. This unsettles Esperanza. She associates few things with her father: his getting up for work in the dark, his thick hands and shoes, the water he combs his hair with and the coffee he drinks. His masculinity, his whole being for her, is encased in the daily rituals that surround his working and the effects of his work. To see her father cry is to view him as a human being as opposed to a breadwinner and an authority figure. She puts her arms around her father and holds him tight, wanting to never let go of this rare moment in which she gets to comfort him. She also recognizes that her father will have to return to Mexico for the funeral. This realization reinforces the notion that she is between two ethnicities, Mexican and American, and in many ways belongs to neither as she negotiates her coming of age. As the eldest child in her family, and because her culture demands this order, it is her job to tell her siblings of their grandmother's death and to keep them quiet out of respect for her father. Gutiérrez-Jones links this moment to the idea that "[t]he continuity between generations will remain unbroken; as her father weeps for the loss of his parent, Esperanza recognizes that some day she will in turn grieve his death—and will herself need to be held and held and held" (303–304). Suddenly, she is forced to face a very tangible mortality.

The notion of respect carries into the next vignette, **"Born Bad,"** as Esperanza relates the most evil deed she has ever committed. The chapter begins with her mother praying for Esperanza because she was born on an evil day. Her friends Lucy and Rachel pray, too, for forgiveness for what they and Esperanza did to Aunt Lupe. Lupe is Esperanza's aunt, a woman formerly beautiful and vibrant, who has been laid low by disease. Esperanza's only knowledge of her aunt outside her sick bed is derived from photos. In the photos her aunt is athletic, a swimmer. Though Esperanza tries, she cannot reconcile the photographs with the reality of her aunt who seems surrounded by a yellow scent, lighting, and bed clothes, as if the illness has infected everything in the room and turned it that sickly hue. Aunt Lupe's illness makes Esperanza consider the nature of good and bad. She lists events she knows only through pictures, trying to imagine the exact instant the illness bloomed in her aunt's body. She includes in her litany of guesses the suggestion that God was busy, too, or what is perhaps the story told by her cousin, that her aunt fell very hard from a high stool. Ultimately, she accepts none of these stories, coming to the difficult assessment that disease is democratic and random. She also muses that sometimes because the disease is so omnipresent, one forgets that things were ever any other way, though Lupe is in grave pain and so close to death.

During one visit to Aunt Lupe, the girls decide to include the ailing woman in a game they play. In the game, they select a famous person to imitate until someone guesses the identity correctly. On this day, the girls decide that it would be fun to choose people from around the neighborhood to imitate rather than celbrities. They decide to imitate Aunt Lupe. Esperanza experiences conflicting feelings because she loves her aunt. Lupe is the only person who listens to every word she says. Esperanza would bring library books and read them to her. In one instance, she tried to show her aunt a picture, holding the book to the woman's face until she tells her niece that she is blind. Esperanza is ashamed, but she returns to the woman's bedside often to share books and even her own poetry. When she finishes reading, her aunt compliments her, and though she is tired, she gives Esperanza the advice that she clings to all her life: "You just remember to keep writing, Esperanza. You must keep writing. It will keep you free." Though Esperanza promises her aunt she will follow the orders, she has no real idea, in that moment, what this will mean for her. Critic Tomoko Kuribayashi suggests that the event is part of a literary heritage: "Her disabled aunt, Lupe, listening to Esperanza's poems, encourages her to keep on writing, her advice embodying the strength Esperanza's culture and older women around her can give her" (172).

Aunt Lupe becomes an iconic figure for Esperanza. Lupe is one of the few women who encourage her to be self-reliant and independent, which makes Esperanza's guilt nearly overwhelming when she and her friends decide to do impressions of her. The girls make themselves limp and cry out for help in weak voices, they pretend to be blind and to have trouble sitting up. What they do not realize is that as they are enjoying their game, Aunt Lupe has died. They are shocked; they had nearly forgotten that the actions they imitated were those of a dying woman. The girls retreat into Catholicism to beg for forgiveness for their actions. Gutiérrez-Jones marks the moment as important in terms of collective experience:

> [t]he girls take on responsibility for her death, and Esperanza unsparingly shoulders her share of the burden for their communal guilt. . . . Such painful encounters with "difference" elucidate Esperanza's encounters with racial prejudice: with misunderstanding and fear born of ignorance, and with the phenomenon of not belonging. (305)

In the next chapter, **"Elenita, Cards, Palm, Water,"** Esperanza goes to the home of the local "witch woman" to have her palm read. Much of the expected mysticism of a fortune teller is missing in this home as Elenita is still a woman with a messy house, needy children, and plastic-covered furniture. Here, the mystical and the sacred co-exist, as both Catholicism and older superstitions are invoked. When Esperanza enters Elenita's home, the fortune teller immediately tells her that today is a better day than yesterday, when the planets were off. Uncertain, Esperanza agrees, and although she is listening to the television in the other room and wants to go watch cartoons like the baby, she chooses not to retreat into the childish activity. Her mission is to discover her future and whether or not it contains a house. They stay in the kitchen where Elenita works between a collection of Catholic paraphernalia and a deck of tarot cards. She tells Esperanza to get the water. On the counter, there are a number of dirty glasses. Esperanza picks the only clean glass, which has a beer logo on it. Elenita asks Esperanza to look into it and tell her what she sees. Esperanza sees nothing. Elenita shrugs it off and makes the sign of the cross over the water three times and cuts the tarot cards. As Elenita works, Esperanza again finds herself distracted by the cartoons on the television. She wants badly to go and watch them, but she stays in the kitchen because she thinks her whole life is "on that kitchen table: past, present, future." Elenita takes Esperanza's hand, looks into it, and closes her eyes. She begins to tell Esperanza what she sees. The most important revelations are the last two: "an anchor of arms" and "a home in the heart." With the anchor, she predicts community to be a part of Esperanza's identity as an adult. With the home in the heart, she predicts that Esperanza's desire to have a house she can be proud of will manifest itself on the interior before she possesses the actual physical structure. Her house is built by the stories and experiences of those around her and by her own compassion and belief in bearing witness to them.

The predictions disappoint Esperanza with their vagueness, particularly in light of the specific magic she knows Elenita is capable of dispensing for other problems like headaches and romantic conundrums. Elenita sees her disappointment and offers to read again, but Esperanza thanks her and gives her five dollars for the job. As they part, Esperanza ponders the meaning of the prediction, and Elenita calls out a good-bye that consists of both the astrological and the sacred, emphasizing again the duality of beliefs in the barrio.

Esperanza is reminded again of Mexico in the next chapter when she tells the story of **"Geraldo No Last Name."** Marin, Esperanza's older neighbor who enchants the boys but is not allowed to leave the yard without permission, goes to dozens of dances in places that Esperanza lists like a litany of forbidden fantasy worlds. The chapter begins with Marin describing an encounter with a man: She met him at a dance, he was young, attractive, and worked in a restaurant. He wore "[G]reen pants and (a) Saturday shirt." Marin continues to explain what happened feeling defensive and self-conscious, asking "And how was she to know that she'd be the last one to see him alive." As she tells the story of the hit-and-run accident that killed him, she makes a point of repeating that she only met him that night, dancing. There is nothing more to connect them except their love of dancing. That is what she told the hospital staff and what she told the police. For all intents and purposes, Geraldo did not exist. He was without identification, without relatives in this country. Marin sat in the emergency room waiting for this man she did not know, though she could not explain why as he was not a boyfriend or even anyone she had met before. Instead, she reduces him to just another new immigrant. She is complicit in marginalizing him, saying "Just another *brazer* who didn't speak English. Just another wetback." Her language mimics that of the police who question her, echoes that of her cousin as she tries to explain what she was doing out at three in the morning. Esperanza, with her own status as a female immigrant, feels empathy for this man who will quickly be forgotten as he belonged to neither the United States or Mexico. She imagines his apartments and the money he sent home—the only tangible evidence he had made it to the United States. When the money ceases, he will be forgotten. There is no structure in place to identify him or to tell his family he is gone. When the money no longer arrives, they will wonder and then agree to give his life over to the country he adopted, ceasing to have any concern for his fate. So, to save him in some small way, Esperanza imagines for him a story. Gutiérrez-Jones believes "She expresses herself as an artist by expressing the struggles of others, establishing her own identity as she conveys the identity of her neighborhood" (307). Esperanza acted out of empathy and the need to represent those who could no longer represent themselves.

"Edna's Ruthie" is yet another disenfranchised person living in the neighborhood. Though she used to write children's books and was once married, she has returned to her mother in a state of childlike innocence. From Esperanza's point of view, she is the only adult she knows who likes to play, and so they play together. Ruthie is the daughter of Edna, the owner of the building next door to Esperanza. She is infamous for her ruthless expulsion of tenants, particularly a pregnant woman she threw out for owning a duck. Esperanza recognizes that Edna would throw Ruthie out as well were she able, but because the young woman is her daughter, she allows her to live there, even though Edna does not show her daughter any affection. Esperanza immediately recognizes the difference between familial duty and love, and in some ways tries to compensate for Edna in her treatment of Ruthie. Ruthie will not enter the candy store with the children, instead she stands outside waiting. If she does go inside, she assumes the look of a trapped animal, suggesting abuse in her past. The children give her candy although her teeth are in poor condition. She repeatedly states that she will go to the dentist the following week. She still possesses the inclinations toward adulthood, but is unable to act upon them. Though the children notice, they choose not to call her on the truth of her comments. She also sees lovely things in everything. Ruthie's ability to see the beauty in life attracts Esperanza to her. Sadly, the experience of beauty is tempered by an inability to make decisions. Esperanza relates the story of when Ruthie is asked to go bowling and a car of people wait for her to make a decision. Ruthie panics and asks her mother who tells her she does not care what Ruthie does. Ruthie remains incapacitated by indecision until the car finally pulls away. That night in support of the woman, the children ask her to play cards and allow her to deal, a tacit way of indicating their sympathy.

Esperanza, though she accepts Ruthie, still wonders why anyone would move to Mango Street if they did not have to. She also wonders where the woman's husband is, even though Ruthie claims she is only visiting and that he will be coming for her. Though the husband never arrives, Esperanza does not judge Ruthie. Husband or no, she is a friend, and Esperanza chooses to give primacy to that. She is such a friend that Esperanza shares her books with Ruthie and even memorizes an entire poem to recite to her, a gift of great distinction to this child of words. She chooses to recite "The Walrus and the Carpenter" by Lewis Carroll, which chronicles the story of the title characters duping a group of young oysters to follow them on a walk, after which they are devoured. Perhaps because of the violent nature of this metric poem, at the end of the recitation, Ruthie looks at Esperanza for a long time and then tells her, "You have the most beautiful teeth I have ever seen," as if perhaps those teeth might eat her.

Esperanza continues describing her neighborhood's residents in **"The Earl of Tennessee."** Earl is yet another neighbor who lives in a basement apartment in Edna's building and works nights. He interacts with the children when he tells them to be quiet and when he gives away portions of his massive collection of damp 45s. As with almost all of the characters in the neighborhood, he is viewed by Esperanza as a combination of good and bad. One of the most remarkable things about the protagonist is her lack of judgment concerning her neighbors. She tells of a wife that Earl is supposed to have and then lists at least three women that the people in the neighborhood suspect is his wife. With each woman, Earl behaves the same: "Whenever she arrives, he holds her tight by the crook of the arm. They walk fast into the apartment, lock the door behind them and don't stay long." As is often the case, Esperanza's narration allows for an objective retelling of significant details that the reader is then required to interpret. Earl's "wives" are prostitutes, despite the euphemistic term of wife applied by the older generation.

"Sire" marks an important turning point in Esperanza's development. In this chapter, she undergoes a rapid sexual metamorphosis. Suddenly, one day, she notices that a boy named Sire is watching her; having someone notice her as a sexual being is both thrilling and frightening for her. As she walks past his house, he stares while he "pitches pennies" with his buddies. Esperanza is determined not to be like some of the other girls, she vows instead to be brave and to walk right past him rather than crossing the street. She even dares to glance at him just once to show that she is not afraid, saying, "I had to look hard, just once, like he was glass. And I did. I did once." The one time was enough to unsettle her, as she stared too long and so transfixed Sire that he rode his bike into a car. She states, "It made your blood freeze to have somebody look at you like that." The experience excites her, makes her feel like she is finally becoming a woman because she has been viewed as one by a curious young man. However, she is not the only one aware of Sire's attentions. Esperanza's father calls him a "punk," and her mother tells her not to talk to him.

The problem is quickly solved when Sire's girlfriend arrives. She is a petite, childlike woman to whom Esperanza compares herself. The girl-woman smells like babies, has little painted toes, and cannot tie her own shoes. Esperanza feels a brief satisfaction that she at least can tie her own shoes, but the shoe tying is merely a trick to get a man to tie it for her, to kneel at her feet and look up at her and be close to her, to make him feel like her protector. Critic Michelle Scalise Sugiyama views "girl-woman" as agreeing to her own submission based on gender roles; she comments,

> This is perhaps best illustrated in the relationship between the tellingly named Sire and his girlfriend, 'tiny and pretty' Lois, who is compared to a baby three times in the same paragraph. We are told not that she and Sire hold hands when they go out on walks, but that *she* holds *his* hand, and that they stop periodically for him to tie her shoes. Whether or not Lois is faking this inability to tie her own shoes, the submission and dependence it results in are quite real (18).

Esperanza, however, still sees it as titillating and romantic. Sometimes Esperanza hears the couple at night laughing and says she can hear the "the trees talking to themselves: wait, wait, wait." She is on the brink of falling in love and becoming a fully sexualized being, and she watches the couple in fascination, hoping to see what will happen to her. The couple leaves for walks together, and Esperanza wonders where he takes her. According to her mother, it is into an alley. The women in the barrio are sometimes equally complicit in judging a woman based on her sexual behavior, and Esperanza's mother is no exception.

Still, the entire relationship and her own sexual identity are unfolding before her eyes, and Esperanza can feel everything in her "holding its breath." She says, "Everything is waiting to explode like Christmas. I want to be all new and shiny. I want to sit out bad at night, a boy around my neck and the wind under my skirt." Esperanza sees her future if she gives into her urges: She will have a boyfriend and she will have the freedom of her newfound maturity, but she will be classified as bad. She also believes that with these newly found sexual urges she will become a whole new person, as if the first years of her life were simply a rehearsal for for the divine being she is to become. Still, perhaps being labeled as bad would be better than the intense longing she feels. She whiles away the hours fixating on Sire, embracing and talking to the trees in her yard and imagining what he and his girlfriend are doing.

In **"Four Skinny Trees,"** Esperanza pays homage to the trees that constitute her confidantes. She relates to them believing that they, like her, are misplaced in the city. They speak to her at night through the window, but it is a special secret because her sister, Nenny, sleeps through the whispers. In an act of intense identification, Esperanza describes the trees as having secret strength: "They send ferocious roots beneath the ground. They grow up and they grow down and grab the earth between their hairy toes and bite the sky with violent teeth and never quit their anger. This is how they keep." Esperanza admires their fierceness and wants it for herself, a sustaining desire that will help her through her shame of living on Mango Street and maintain her desire for a real house. The trees represent sheer perseverance against the harsh challenges of the city. They call to her: "Keep, keep, keep, trees say when I sleep. They teach." Their lesson is determination, and when Esperanza fears that she will forget to stay true to this family and their message, she stares at the branches that continue to reach into the sky despite their surroundings.

"No Speak English" is a critical chapter as well, for the way in which Esperanza describes the experience of an immigrant in her neighborhood. Contrary to the traditional view of the immigrant striving to come to the United States in pursuit of the American Dream, Mamacita comes because her husband sends for her. In Chicago, he works two jobs, saves his money, and sends for his wife and child in Mexico. When they finally come, Esperanza is fascinated by the woman from the start. When Mamacita extends her dainty foot from the cab, its tiny proportions and pink color seem beautiful, even as Esperanza views the thick ankle and finally the entire woman as she is pushed and pulled from the taxi by her husband and the driver. As Esperanza describes it, "All at once she bloomed. Huge, enormous, beautiful to look at, from the salmon-pink feather on the tip of her hat to the little rosebuds of her shoes." Esperanza views the woman as a greenhouse flower of sorts, and the woman fulfils the image because she remains forever in the apartment and forever foreign to the inhabitants of the neighborhood.

Esperanza emphasizes the tiny feet and the unlikely woman that they support. The reference to shoes again suggests the ways women are cloistered in the novel, as the critic Michelle Scalise Sugiyama suggests (12). Some say the woman does not come down from the apartment because she is too fat, others say that she she cannot descend and then climb the stairs again, but the ever-attentive Esperanza believes it is because she cannot speak English and, without language, Mamacita will remain forever excluded from her new culture. Esperanza's father reinforces this belief when he remembers that the only words that he spoke when he came to the United States were "hamandeggs." He ordered it for every meal as it was the only English he knew. When Esperanza says now he no longer has ham and eggs, it is clear that her father has made the crucial linguistic transition necessary to become a citizen of the United States.

Although Mamacita does not come out of the apartment, the neighbors know that she is in there from the homesick songs she sings as she listens to the Spanish radio shows. Her homesickness is so intense that her husband paints the interior of the apartment pink, like the house that she left, but it is not enough. Mamacita is still racked with a longing for her homeland. She cries for her former life, and her husband becomes angry and yells at her, telling her that they are home. Esperanza describes the effect of his words: "¡A! *Mamacita*, who does not belong, every once in a while lets out a cry, hysterical, high, as if he had torn the only skinny thread that kept her alive, the only road to that country." Esperanza describes it so well because she closely associates with Mamacita's feelings of dislocation and powerlessness over her situation. Mamacita is at the mercy of her husband's desires and must live where he dictates. She is ultimately forced to accept her new life when her baby boy begins talking and sings the Pepsi commercial he heard on television. Recognizing that her life in Mexico is over, she begs the baby not to become American, not to adopt English, the "tinny, harsh" language. She cries out to him, "No, no, no, as if she can't believe her ears."

In **"Rafaela Who Drinks Coconut & Papaya Juice on Tuesdays,"** we see another woman at the mercy of a man. Rafaela gets locked indoors when her husband comes home because he believes she might run away since "she is too beautiful to look at." Clearly her beauty makes her a sexually powerful presence in the neighborhood. He seeks to contain that power. As a result, Rafaela must ask the neighborhood kids to get her papaya juice or coconut juice. She sends down the money on a string, and the kids return with her request, tie it to the string, and she pulls it up into her room. Rafaela, too, is displaced from her youth, from dancing and having fun; instead, she leans out the window longing to be independent, to "throw green eyes easily like dice and open homes with keys." She believes that with her freedom and her sexual power, life would be better, less bitter. Still, the brief vignette ends with the idea of "someone promising to keep them on a silver string." Even her visions of freedom culminate in a man giving her freedom, not in her own self-sufficiency.

"Sally," the title character of the chapter, is a friend of Esperanza's, a beautiful girl whose father is overbearing in his protection of his daughter's virginity. According to Esperanza, Sally's father claims that "to be this beautiful is trouble," another suggestion that danger comes from a woman's sexual power and a man's predatory nature. Her father excuses his behavior based on the severity of his religion. He fears that his daughter will become like his sisters, who, it is intimated, fell from grace and shamed the family. However, for Esperanza, Sally is exotic and sexual, someone from whom she might learn to control her own burgeoning sexual power. Esperanza asks Sally questions about beauty tricks. Unlike Sally, Esperanza has a mother who watches carefully over everything she wears: no nylons, no black shoes, and no make-up. Mrs. Cordero claims that "to wear black so young is dangerous." Again, the notion of danger and sexuality are closely linked.

For Esperanza and for others, Sally proves to be a dangerous friend. Sally loses her best friend after trying to pierce her ears. The incident results in a fight where Sally gets bitten by the friend and called a name. Bravely, Sally refuses to cry, but Esperanza knows that this loss is a painful one, leaving Sally without someone to confide in and share with. Esperanza's sense of empathy is so intense that she defends Sally in the telling of the story, adamantly stating that the stories the boys tell in the coatroom are not true. Again, the suggestion is that these stories are about Sally's sexual permissiveness and Esperanza chooses to defend her as she sees Sally become two different people between school and the neighborhood. Before Sally goes home, she wipes off her make-up and straightens her skirt, becoming the perfect daughter for her father who locks her in the house. Esperanza wonders if Sally ever wishes she did not have to go home, if the girl ever wants to move to another house. In considering the possibility, Esperanza projects her own desires onto Sally. Suddenly in her attempt to articulate Sally's desire, she is expressing her own:

There'd be no nosy neighbors watching, no motorcycles and cars, no sheets and towels and laundry. Only trees and more trees and plenty of blue sky. And you could laugh, Sally. You could go to sleep and wake up and never have to think of who likes and doesn't like you. You could close your eyes and you wouldn't have to worry what people said because you never belonged here anyway and nobody could make you sad and nobody would think you're strange because you like to dream and dream. And no one could yell at you if they saw you out in the dark leaning against a car, leaning against somebody without someone thinking you are bad, without somebody saying it is wrong, without the whole world waiting for you to make a mistake when all you wanted, all you wanted, Sally, was to love and to love and to love and to love, and no one could call that crazy. (83)

In this moment of reverie, Esperanza expresses all of the things that she feels imprison her on Mango Street: the environment itself, the repressive social code, the nosy neighbors, the lack of dreams, the suffocating gender stratification that maligns sexual women, and the lack of openness. Gutiérrez-Jones asserts, "In particular, Esperanza grasps Sally's unhappiness, and shares with her the anguish of a home that can never fulfill that term's promise—a home which is not her own, a home where 'she never belonged . . . anyway'" (304). On a technical note, the rhythm that Cisneros builds in her prose directly mirrors the rhythms of Esperanza's desire.

In **"Minerva Writes Poems,"** Esperanza sees to a certain degree how the desire for a man too early can result in a life of misery. Minerva is only a little older than Esperanza, and she has two children, an unstable marriage, and an abusive husband. Esperanza and Minerva exchange poems with each other. Minerva fits her creative life in around her children and her husband, a caution to Esperanza who wants to give her writing primacy in life. Writing is becoming, as Elenita the witch woman foretold, the home within Esperanza's heart. Minerva's marriage also enhances Esperanza's wariness of men, as Minerva's husband "who left and keeps leaving" returns home to find his belongings thrown out of the house. He beats his wife in response, then apologizes and she lets him back in. Esperanza watches Minerva enact and accept her role as the abused wife, as she allows her husband and the suffering he brings with him to rule both her actual and creative life. After her husband returns, she asks Esperanza, "what can (I) do?" Esperanza is defeated by the situation, unable to help her friend and unable to foresee what will happen in Minerva's future. She ends the chapter saying, "There is nothing I can do." Esperanza has given up on helping Minerva, who has given up on saving herself. They are both worn down by the circumstances.

Still, Esperanza maintains her desire to help people despite her experience with Minerva. In **"Bums in the Attic,"** she explains the humanitarian aspect of her fantasy house, a notion developed after Sunday drives she took with her family to look at the gardens of the rich people for whom her father works. When she announces that she no longer wants to go on these rides, her father assumes it is because she is "getting too old" for it. Her sister Nenny suggests it is because Esperanza is "getting too stuck up." What Esperanza does not tell them is that she is ashamed, "all of us staring out the window like the hungry. I'm tired of looking at what we can't have. When we win the lottery . . . Mama begins, and then I stop listening." Esperanza feels distanced from her family and disillusioned, too old to believe in the family dream of the lottery or some other divine intervention. She realizes that whatever comes to them must be earthbound, from the hard work or generosity of one committed person. When she looks at the houses on the hills, she recognizes that the people who live in those houses are too content with their own affluence to look at what other people need, that they fear nothing and know nothing of what goes on in the neighborhoods below them. Their willful ignorance makes Esperanza vow: "One day I'll own my own house, but I won't forget who I am or where I came from." She determines to let the homeless have the attic of her house, where they will be safe. She pledges this as she will always remember what it means to have the house and to have gone without it. She envisions herself sitting by the fire with guests and explaining the creaking floorboards to friends, "Bums, I'll say and I'll be happy."

Esperanza continues to blaze her own path of liberation in **"Beautiful and Cruel**." She names herself the ugly daughter, the one "nobody comes for." It is the beauty of the woman, she believes, that makes the suitor come to take her away. Her sister Nenny on the other hand is pretty. Nenny says that "she won't wait her whole life for a husband to come and get her." The girl notes that a neighbor left Mango Street by having a baby, but Nenny does not want that to be her means of escape either. She wants to pick and choose her mate. Esperanza thinks it is easy for Nenny to make these decisions because her younger sister is the pretty sort of girl that men desire. Esperanza's mother notices her older daughter's jealousy and tells her that when she gets older her "dusty hair will settle" and her "blouse will learn to stay clean," but even in the midst of this reassurance, Esperanza remains unconvinced that this is actually what she wants. Rather, she vows "not to grow up tame like the others who lay their necks on the threshold waiting for the ball and chain." She decides that whatever fate has in store for her, she will be in control of it. She thinks of movies in which "there is always one with red red lips who is beautiful and cruel." This woman controls the men around her with her sexuality, and she refuses to give that power away. Esperanza chooses to be that woman, to take control of her power. She begins her campaign quietly, by leaving "the table like a man, without putting back the chair or picking up the plate." She realizes that to have power, she has to seize it and actively work to break down gender codes, and she begins with the table.

To further illustrate the purpose of her resistance to the status quo, Esperanza explains the regrets of her mother in **"A Smart Cookie."** Her mother laments what she might have been if she had not given in to cultural norms and gotten married and had children. Her mother is multitalented: She sings opera, knows how to fix the television, speaks two languages, makes beautiful pieces with needle and thread, but is unable to function outside the barrio. The city, though she has lived there her whole life, defeats and intimidates her. Though she wants to see a play, a ballet, an opera, she does nothing to create these experiences for herself, instead living vicariously by singing along with opera albums borrowed from the library. What is perhaps most moving about Mrs. Cordero is that she knows she has given up her life. She tells her daughter to study hard and to rely solely on herself, citing other women whose husbands have left, leaving them with nothing. She says, "Got to take care all your own." Then she follows her outburst with a few last words, explaining to Esperanza that she left school due to shame over her old clothes. She urges her daughter to not accept shame but to rise above it and choose her life, rather than choosing to be subjugated because of social appearances and public opinion.

The threat of the abusive male continues in **"What Sally Said."** The chapter begins with Sally rationalizing her father's abuse, "He never hits me hard." Regardless of her claim, her mother has to rub the places it hurts with lard, and Sally has to lie about the abuse when she goes to school, claiming she fell to explain all of the bruises and scars. No one, particularly not Esperanza, is fooled. Sally is too old to be so clumsy, and the claim that he never hits her hard lies in direct opposition to her swollen and bruised face. One day, as Sally describes it, "he hit her with his hands just like a dog." According to Sally, his motivation stems from the fact that she is a daughter, who might run away like his own sisters did, thereby shaming the family. After this incident, Sally gets permission to stay with Esperanza's family. She brings with her some clothes and a pathetic offering of a sweetbread from her powerless mother. That night her father comes to the house, having been crying, to beg his daughter to come home, claiming the physical abuse will not happen again. Then, Esperanza believes there is nothing more to worry about until, a few days later, Sally's father sees her talking to a boy. Over the next few days, Sally doesn't come to school. Her father beat her with his belt, "[U]ntil the way Sally tells it, he just went crazy, he just forgot he was her father between the buckle and the belt." Afterwards he repeats to himself: "You're not my daughter, you're not my daughter" and then weeps. It is hard to tell if part of his self-loathing is based on sexual abuse or if it is solely physical abuse. In either case, he reinforces the pattern of men and violence, particularly within domestic spaces, that factors so prominently in the world of the book.

Sally is in trouble again in **"The Monkey Garden,"** but this time the trouble is of her own making. The monkey garden was formerly inhabited by a family with a mean monkey that bit and screeched. Once the family left, the children of the neighborhood begin to take over the garden as a place to play, imagining that it had been there since time began. Within a few months after the former tenants had moved out, the garden begins to reclaim itself, growing over bricks and boundaries. Cars were abandoned there, and the garden grew over them as well. This wild abundance in some ways the Garden of Eden, particularly with the sexual awakening that will occur there. Esperanza plays with the other children, climbing through the cars until she realizes that Sally is missing. When she goes to look for her friend, she sees that Tito and his friends have stolen Sally's keys and have conceived of a game wherein they will only return the keys to her if she kisses them. Immediately, Esperanza knows that this is a dangerous game. Though she cannot articulate exactly what she objects to, something in her knows that bartering sexual favors is not right. In her panic, she runs up to Tito's apartment and tells his mother who laughs it off as childish mischief. Determined to save her friend on her own, Esperanza gathers three sticks and a brick to beat the boys off, convinced that Sally wants to be saved from the power-mongering boys.

When Esperanza arrives on the scene with her arsenal, Sally tells her to go home. The boys also tell her to leave them alone, and Esperanza feels shame over what the other adolescents have made her feel is her overreaction. She hides in the jungle of the monkey garden, where she can cry without being seen. Her shame is so great that she tries to will her heart to stop beating like the Indian priests she has read about. The event causes Esperanza to lose the garden. Like the Garden of Eden, the acquiring of knowledge has caused it to be lost forever, only in this role reversal, Esperanza is the Adam character seduced by her friendship with Sally into uncovering knowledge she does not really want to possess. Critic Ellen McCracken links this story with others ("What Sally Said," "Red Clowns") in what she deems the "Sally cycle" in which Esperanza begins to make powerful connections between "sex, male power, and violence in patriarchal society" (69).

In **"Red Clowns"** Sally again causes hurt to Esperanza. In the beginning of the chapter, Esperanza sounds desperate and betrayed, insisting "Sally, you lied. It wasn't what you said at all. What he did. Where he touched me. I didn't want it, Sally. The way they said it, the way it's supposed to be, all the storybooks and movies, why did you lie to me?" Esperanza is sexually assaulted by an older boy at the carnival, an act that radically transforms her bookish ideas of love and sexual pleasure. At the heart of the assault is Sally, who was supposed to meet Esperanza by the clowns but fails to do so. Esperanza waits, wondering where the older boy that Sally left with has taken her. While waiting for her friend, a group of boys approaches Esperanza, one grabs her arm and says, "I love you, Spanish girl, I love you." His use of her ethnicity to name and identify her suggests that he is white. The boys sexually assault her, and Esperanza is powerless to do anything but scream until eventually she can only cry. She feels betrayed on multiple levels by Sally who does not come to save her, by all of the lies that she has heard about sexual pleasure, by waiting her whole life for a moment that turns out to be both painful and ugly. Critic Maria Herrera-Sobek articulates the betrayal in terms of the community:

> The diatribe is directed not only at Sally the silent interlocutor but at the community of women who keep the truth from the younger generation of women in a conspiracy of silence. The protagonist discovers a conspiracy of two forms of silence: silence in not denouncing the "real" facts of life about sex and its negative aspects in violent sexual encounters, and complicity in embroidering a fairy-tale-like mist around sex, and romanticizing and idealizing unrealistic sexual relations (252).

The effect of silence is part of Esperanza's shame and need to deny the assault when she begs Sally not to make her tell what happened in its entirety. All of Esperanza's innocent pleasure in her sexual awakening is shattered in this moment, and her friendship with Sally is irrevocably destroyed.

"Linoleum Roses" documents the seemingly inevitable. Sally marries a salesman she meets at the school bazaar and moves to another state where it is legal to get married before the eighth grade. She claims to be happy because she can buy things now, but her husband has violent tendencies like her father and, though she claims that she left for love, Esperanza believes Sally married the salesman to escape. Her husband keeps her locked tight in the house. She cannot look out the window or talk on the telephone, and friends are not allowed to visit unless he is away. In the final moment of the chapter, Sally sits inside the house looking at all of the things that they own, never realizing that she is one more owned object among them.

In **"The Three Sisters,"** Cisneros writes of three elderly aunts from Mexico. Critic Maria Elena de Valdés links them to a number of traditions:

> In pre-Hispanic Mexico, the lunar goddesses, such as Tlazolteotl and Xochiquetzal, were the intermediaries for all women (Westheim 105). They are sisters to each other and, as women, sisters to Esperanza.... At the symbolic level, the sisters are linked with Clotho, Lachesis, and Atropos, the three fates.... In Cisneros's text, the prophecy of the fates turn to the evocation of self-knowledge. (58)

The revelatory women are great aunts of Lucy and Rachel's, and they come after the death of the girls' baby sibling. The child dies after a series of signs: a dog's cry and bird flying into an open window. At the funeral, everyone comes to look at the house and to pray for the baby Esperanza describes as "that little thumb of a human in a box like candy." For Esperanza, the rituals of the wake are new and unsettling. As she stands in the room uncertain of what to do, the three old sisters call her over to them. Esperanza feels trepidation but relaxes when she identifies their collective scent as that of "Kleenex or the inside of a satin handbag." The three sisters ask Esperanza her name, and she answers them. One of the sisters comments that Esperanza's name is "good," another says that her knees hurt, it will rain tomorrow. Esperanza wants to know how they can predict the weather, but the women simply say, "We know." Then they look at her hands and become animated, murmuring among themselves that Esperanza will "go very far." They tell the girl to make a wish. Esperanza asks to make sure there are no limits to this wish, and they assure her there are not, so she immediately wishes for her own house. When she is finished, the women assure her that it will come true.

Again, Esperanza asks how they know, and they reiterate, "We know, we know." Then, the woman with what are described as marble hands pulls Esperanza aside, takes her face between her palms and tells her, "When you leave you must remember to always come back." Immediately, Esperanza is baffled and a little afraid, believing the woman has read her mind. The old woman repeats, "When you leave you must remember to come back for the others. A circle, understand? You will always be Esperanza. You will always be Mango Street. You can't erase what you know. You can't forget who you are." Esperanza is both spooked and speechless from the woman's insight. The old woman continues, explaining that others will not be able to leave as easily as she, that she must respect them and come back to help. Esperanza promises to remember the words of the woman who dismisses Esperanza to go play with Lucy and Rachel. To enhance the strangeness and portent of the experience, Esperanza never sees the women again.

The women become, in their own way, members of the circle of women that surrounds Esperanza. These women encourage her with words, like her mother, Ruthie, and Aunt Lupe; they teach through example like Sally, Alicia, and Minerva; they share experience like Minerva, Mamacita, Lucy, and Rachel; and they offer futures like Elenita. Within this circle, Esperanza becomes the conduit for their stories and their wisdom. Like many Chicanas, she carries the history of the community with her and learns from it. She also bears witness to the lives of the people of Mango Street.

In **"Alicia and I Talking on Edna's Steps,"** Esperanza gains additional insight. Alicia gives Esperanza a bag from her home, Guadalajara, which she treasures. Alicia's dream is the opposite of Esperanza's. She does not want to move toward a place unknown, she wants to return to the place that she knows best, her home in Mexico. Esperanza confides in Alicia her disappointment over not having a house. A little baffled, Alicia points to the house on Mango Street, asking Esperanza whether or not this is her home. Esperanza denies it is her own: "No this isn't my house I say and shake my head as if shaking could undo the year I've lived here. I don't belong. I don't ever want to come from here." Desperate to be understood, she invokes Alicia's situation of having a home to return to where she can be happy and can belong. Alicia forces her to face the reality: "No, Alicia says. Like it or not you are Mango Street and one day you'll come back too." Esperanza denies this, saying she will not return until Mango Street is better. Alicia laughs at the idea, wondering who would ever try to make it better, emphasizing again how forgotten and disenfranchised the neighborhood really is. She and Esperanza joke that maybe the mayor will do it, but the conversation sets Esperanza wondering who will actually come to Mango Street. She is slowly coming to believe that the duty may perhaps fall to her. The critic McCracken links this discussion to Esperanza's comments on bums in the attic: "She conceives of a house as a communal rather than private property; such sharing runs counter to the dominant ideological discourse that strongly affects consciousness in capitalist societies." (64) Again, the emphasis on the individual is minimal when compared to the communal whole.

In the next chapter, **"A House of My Own,"** there is a sense of lineage between Esperanza's chapter and Virginia Woolf's *A Room of One's Own*. Both women are struggling to have space for their writing and a right to control their own lives. Esperanza dreams of a house that is not an apartment and that, more importantly, is "Not a man's house. Not a daddy's." Instead it is only hers. Gutiérrez-Jones sees this as a rejection of male traditions, and Jacqueline Doyle believes the wish is in keeping with Virginia Woolf's desire for *A Room of One's Own*. Esperanza determines to make the house beautiful with flowers and books, where her things stay where they are left and no one interferes or judges her decisions. She wants "Only a house quiet as snow, a space for myself to go, clean as paper before the poem." Each item in her list references the notion of possibility. With this house, she will have the opportunity to do whatever she would like, unlike in the barrio at large, where the opportunities are limited by income, gender, language, and ethnicity.

In the final chapter of the book, **"Mango Says Goodbye Sometimes,"** nearly a year after the beginning, Esperanza has finally begun to build the house of the heart that Elenita foretold in her kitchen. Esperanza writes about how she likes to tell stories, to narrate her own life as she lives it. She begins to tell the story of her house on Mango Street, returning to some of the language that began the book. The act of writing frees Esperanza from the memory of the house where she belongs but does "not belong to." Writing allows her to say good-bye to Mango Street, to release the most haunting aspects of her past. These first pages of her story tell her that she will be able to eventually bid farewell to Mango Street forever. She imagines her friends and neighbors gossiping and wondering where it is she has gone and why she has to go so far away. Esperanza keeps the secret of her strength, "They will not know I have gone away to come back. For the ones I left behind. For the ones who cannot get out." Esperanza must find the place and privacy within her where she can write and free herself from the memory of Mango Street. In so doing, she will liberate the others by telling their stories. Critic Yvonne Yarbro-Bejarano defines what will become Esperanza's legacy: "Writing has been essential in connecting her with the power of women and her promise to pass down that power to other women is fulfilled by the writing and the publication of the text itself" (217). The very act of circling back to the language of the beginning of the book suggests that Esperanza has, in fact, begun to bring the story to paper and obviously to print. This self-conscious move reinforces the act of writing as a mode of bearing witness for the many disenfranchised individuals who appear throughout *The House on Mango Street*.

Critical Views

JOSEPH SOMMERS ON THREE CRITICAL APPROACHES TO CHICANO LITERATURE

Of the three main lines of critical approach to Chicano literature, the most prominent in academic publications is that which attempts to apply the norms and categories of formalist criticism. It seeks to validate Chicano texts, for both Chicano and Anglo readers, as authentic modern literature.

The methodology varies, but the two most common features are reliance on comparative criteria and stress on textual analysis. Some comparatists focus on identifying literary influences (for example, Juan Rulfo on Tomás Rivera), tending to base their claims for the validity of the Chicano text on its derivation from sources of recognized excellence. Others refer to established definitions such as "modernism" to call attention to what for them is a "newly emerged" literature. Textual critics try to show that the criteria of stylistics and more recently of structuralist criticism can reveal in a Chicano poem or narrative the types of complexity and levels of formal coherence which are found in exemplary texts of modern literature. Other critics such as Juan Bruce-Novoa retain the formalist insistence on separating the text from historical reality or social context, but nonetheless seek to account for "meaning." This approach to "meaning" limits it to the realm of the imaginary, postulating the text as occupying "imaginary space,"[2] as being mental experience which provides an alternative to lived experience, to the chaos, injustice and temporality of the real world. Meaning rather than reference to reality, becomes yet another index of the literariness of the work.

What underlying assumptions characterize this approach to a given text? For one, emphasis on accepted major works as models carries the assumption that literature is a phenomenon of print, with the most respected exemplars being those valued by the educated middle class. A corollary assumption attaches relatively low value to oral literature, the product of a popular culture which introduces collective themes based on concrete experience, which relies upon oral transmission, which is frequently anonymous, and which historically has provided a source of resistance to the dominant ideology.[3] A second corollary is stress on the text as individualized creation. In this view, the act of literary production is the artist's private struggle to find a personal voice and to express an individualized response. The poet is seen as arbitrarily gifted with the quality of genius, as being endowed with special intuitive insights and access to the truth.

A further assumption is that the prime feature of a literary text is its aesthetic quality, which cannot be measured by the yardstick of meaning or cognition, for these are categories which normally rest upon criteria of reason and of reference to experienced reality. Aesthetic quality on the other hand can be uncovered by analysis of features contained within the text, features which when taken together yield "unity" and "complexity."

Finally there is a widespread tendency to value the quality of "universality." This quality is rarely defined, except by implication or by negation. Some critics seem to state that to be universal is somehow to transcend "social protest" (presumably they would strike Galdós, Neruda and the entire picaresque novel from the "universal" list). Others seem to suggest that literature achieves universality by avoiding the regional or the immediately historical in favor of the abstract, the metaphysical, the imaginary, or the timeless themes and myths of world culture (this would underestimate the importance of regional themes and historical issues in Balzac, Tolstoy, Malraux and the corpus of Spanish epic poetry). What seems involved beneath the surface of these notions is a fragmentation of categories which might otherwise be seen as interconnected, such as the artistic and the social, or the imaginary and the historical. Certainly one can infer from this view of universality a conception of literature as distraction, or as aesthetic object, or as distinct mode of mental activity from other disciplines, or as embodied in a succession of masterpieces insulated against the ravages of time by protective jackets of brilliant thematic colors.

What are the consequences when these assumptions constitute the critic's point of departure? On the positive side is a healthy stress on intensive analysis of the formal qualities of given texts. On the negative side, the bulk of this type of criticism tends to be ahistorical, concentrating on contemporary texts and their modernism. By extension this has meant a thrust toward the assimilation of Chicano literature, or more precisely of a select number of Chicano texts, into the standard reading list of the educated reader, primarily in academe. The critic's role, when these assumptions are primary, is, as Bruce-Novoa phrased it, "to lead the reader back to the literary work itself,"[4] for literature in this view constitutes a separate, non-referential transcendental reality.

The second line of critical approach, prominent during the 1960s, is based on the notion of *cultural uniqueness*. It values Chicano literature precisely because in it one finds expression of the distinctive features of Chicano culture. An earlier philologically oriented but nonetheless culturalist variant, practiced by Aurelio Espinosa half a century ago, stressed the survival of authentic Spanish forms in the Southwest.

The critical methodology tends to stress descriptive cultural features: family structures, linguistic and thematic survivals, anti-gringo attitudes, pre-Hispanic symbology, notions of a mythic past, and folk beliefs ranging from *la llorona* to the Virgin of Guadalupe. Some culturalist critics, waging a necessary struggle against the elitism which characterizes purist notions of literary Spanish, stress the distinguishing presence in Chicano literature of what sociolinguists term code-switching and what critics have called the binary phenomenon—a process by which linguistic symbols and syntactic structures of two languages interact in the same text. Others stress the presence of Aztec symbols or myths. Thus Herminio Rios and Octavio Romano find special value in *Bless Me Ultima*, the novel by Rudolfo Anaya, because, "It is from our collective memory that he draws myths such as that of Cihuacoatl. . . . And it is from our collective subconscious that the myth of the Golden Carp arises . . . Anaya takes us from the subconscious to the conscious, from the past to the present . . . in so doing, he has helped us to know ourselves."[5]

What assumptions underlie culturalist criticism? One is evident in attributing positive value to Anaya because his novel reveals traces of the Aztec world view. Stated in bare terms, it claims that present-day Chicano mental structures, by dint of a sort of Jungian operation of the collective unconscious, retain continuity with the thought patterns and cosmology of the Aztec past. Also implied is the notion that rediscovery of cultural origins imparts a healthy consciousness of uniqueness to the generations of the present. This notion that the distant past—and here I refer to a mythic, magical past rather than to the past in a historical process of change—shapes and controls the present, regardless of social and historical developments, is by no means original. A Mexican example embodying the same anti-historical view is the essay by Octavio Paz, *Posdata*,[6] in which the well known Mexican poet and critic attempts to explain the Tlatelolco massacre of 1968 in terms of the persistence of pre-Hispanic values and attitudes. Comparable manifestations of this cultural pessimism can be found in the creative works of Carlos Fuentes, *La región más transparente* and *Todos los gatos son pardos*, as well as his essays, *Tiempo mexicano*.[7] It was this ingredient in Chicano thought which led Philip Ortego to state in 1971: "Perhaps the principal significance of the Chicano Renaissance lies in the identification of Chicanos with their Indian past."[8]

There are other related assumptions which form part of the matrix of culturalist thought. One is the positive value attached to tradition regardless of its content. For example, the traditional role of the church, whether in its mystical or its adaptive manifestations, is seen as integral to Chicano culture. A further tendency is to criticize the materialism, racism, and dehumanisation of contemporary capitalist society by counterposing idealistically the values of traditional culture, presenting these values as flawless and recoverable in unchanged form. Needless to say this thesis construes culture to be static and separable from the historic process, rather than dynamic, creative and responsive to experience.

58

Another notion of culturalist thought, embedded in the Plan de Aztlán, places primacy on the distinctive ethnic origins of Chicano culture, setting it apart from other cultures and indeed from other nations. Here the stress is on racial fusion, on Indian and Mexican constituent elements, with occasional references to a Hispano component. There is frequent harking back to José Vasconcelos' slogan, "la raza cósmica," and to *mestizaje* as being the distinctive feature characterizing the Chicano experience. The key assumptions here not only view culture as static, but also view race (and ultimately nature and the biological process) as the controlling element in culture, while positing culture as the central determinant of a people's experience. This line of thought tends to subordinate the idea that culture might be related to the social category of class, as well is the idea that cultural forms evolve in response to the specifics of the historical process. The upshot for critical practice is usually the adoption of one of the several variants of "myth criticism" which have been in vogue in academe recently, centered on archetypal qualities in human nature and archetypal patterns in human relations.

A further implicit assumption in some culturalist criticism, not in consonance with myth criticism, is that Chicano literature can be understood only by Chicanos and interpreted only by Chicanos. In this view Chicano critics writing from a Chicano perspective and publishing in Chicano periodicals are the only reliable sources of understanding of Chicano literature.[9] Accompanying this assumption is the idea that all literary expression by Chicanos constitutes a contribution to the body of Chicano culture. This assumes that *lo chicano* is good by definition, thus eliminating the critical function of literary criticism.

The consequences of such an approach are reductive. It conceives of Chicano literature as ethnic literature, designed for and limited to an ethnic readership, to be isolated academically within ethnic studies programs. It supposes that Chicano literature is distinct from other literatures which may in fact have comparable structural features (such as an oral tradition or the bilingual mode or historical trajectories involving confrontation with class exploitation and institutional racism). It abandons the struggle to redefine exclusivist views of American literature. And finally, whereas formalism tends to ignore the past, focusing on modernism and its virtues, a culturalist approach tends to ignore the present, stressing in nostalgic and idealized terms the predominance of the past.

The third line of critical approach, espoused by this critic, rejects the classic distinction sanctified by René Wellek and Austin Warren between "intrinsic" and "extrinsic"[10] in favor of a criticism that is historically based and dialectically formulated. For the label-minded it can include the work of Marxists but is not practiced exclusively by Marxist critics. The working definition of "literary criticism," in this view, is ample and complex. It begins by explaining the singular formal qualities of a text which distinguish it from alternate modes of verbal expression. It must also account for the manner in which a given text rejects, modifies and incorporates features of other texts which have preceded it. Analysis, then, includes the notion of intertextuality, the response to literary tradition. Since the critic sees literature as a cultural product, the text is also studied in relation to its cultural ambience, which means in the light of an understanding of societal structures.

Finally the critic assumes that to experience literary texts, even in their most fantastic and abstract variants, is a form of cognition, for the text comments upon, refers to and interprets human experience.

Treating critical approaches dialectically, the critic does not reject formalism or culturalist analysis out of hand, but tries to incorporate their positive features into a system which transcends their self-imposed limitations. Hence this third approach incorporates into its methodology the concerns of the sociology of literature, which range from analyzing the material conditions and the intellectual climate of literary production to interpreting the reception and the impact of a given text. Another dialectical aspect of this approach is its attempt to identify an internal Chicano literary dynamic and simultaneously to account for interactions with both

Mexican and North American middle class and popular literary traditions.

Notes

2. This is a central notion in his "The Space of Chicano Literature," *De colores* (Albuquerque), I, 4 (Winter, 1975), pp. 22–42.

3. Arturo Islas seems to imply this assumption of low value in "Writing from a Dual Perspective, *Miquiztli*" (Stanford University), II, 1 (Winter, 1974), p. 2: "More often than not, much of the fiction we do have is document, and sometimes not very well written document. Much of what is passed off as literature is a compendium of folklore, religious superstition, and recipes for tortillas. All well and good, but it is not literature."

4. "The Space of Chicano Literature," p. 39.

5. "Introduction", *Bless Me Ultima* (Berkeley: Quinto Sol, 1972), p. ix.

6. (México: Siglo XXI, 1970).

7. (México: Joaquín Mortiz, 1971).

8. "Chicano Poetry: Roots and Writers," in *New Voices in Literature: The Mexican American.* A Symposium. (Edinburg, Texas: Dept. of English, 1971), p. 11.

9. I do *not* intend in my own departure from culturalist thought to imply that non-Chicano critics will have just as much light to shed as Chicano critics. I would suggest that while Chicano critics' insights are indispensable in the interpretation of key texts, particularly in regard to cultural meanings, symbols, and nuances, the contributions of other critics may be useful, particularly in establishing the extra-cultural merits and significance of such texts.

10. This distinction underlies the entire structure of their important volume, *Theory of Literature* (New York: Harcourt Brace, 2nd ed., 1956).

ELLEN MCCRACKEN ON CISNEROS'S PLACE IN THE AMERICAN LITERATURE CANON

Introspection has achieved a privileged status in bourgeois literary production, corresponding to the ideological emphasis on individualism under capitalism, precisely as the personal and political power of many real individuals has steadily deteriorated. In forms as diverse as European Romantic poetry, late nineteenth-century Modernismo in Latin America, the poetry of the Mexican Contemporáneos of the 1930s, the early twentieth-century modernistic prose of a Proust, the French *nouveau roman*, and other avant-garde texts that take pride in an exclusionary hermeticism, the self is frequently accorded exaggerated importance in stark contrast to the actual position of the individual in the writer's historical moment. Critical readers of these texts are, of course, often able to compensate for the writer's omissions, positioning the introspective search within the historical dimension and drawing the text into the very socio-political realm that the writer has tried to avoid. Nonetheless, many of us, at one time or another, are drawn into the glorified individualism of these texts, experiencing voyeuristic and sometimes identificatory pleasure as witnesses of another's search for the self, or congratulating ourselves on the mental acuity we possess to decode such a difficult and avant-garde text.

Literary critics have awarded many of these texts canonical status. As Terry Eagleton has argued, theorists, critics, and teachers are "custodians of a discourse" and select certain texts for inclusion in the canon that are "more amenable to this discourse than others."[1] Based on power, Eagleton suggests metaphorically, literary criticism sometimes tolerates regional dialects of the discourse but not those that sound like another language altogether: "To be on the inside of the discourse itself is to be blind to this power, for what is more natural and non-dominative than to speak one's own tongue?"

The discourse of power to which Eagleton refers here is linked to ideology as well. The regional dialects of criticism that are accepted must be compatible, ideologically as well as semantically, with the dominant discourse. Criticism, for example, that questions the canonical status of the introspective texts mentioned above, or suggests admission to the canon of texts that depart from such individualistic notions of the self, is often labeled pejoratively or excluded from academic institutions and publication avenues. . . .

The specific example to which I refer, Sandra Cisneros' *The House on Mango Street*, was published by a small regional press in 1984 and reprinted in a second edition of 3,000 in 1985.[2] Difficult to find in most libraries and bookstores, it is well known among Chicano critics and scholars, but virtually unheard of in larger academic and critical circles. In May 1985 it won the Before Columbus Foundation's American Book Award,[3] but this prize has not greatly increased the volume's national visibility. Cisneros' book has not been excluded from the canon solely because of its publishing circumstances: major publishing houses are quick to capitalize on a Richard Rodríguez whose widely distributed and reviewed *Hunger of Memory* (1982) does not depart ideologically and semantically from the dominant discourse. They are even willing to market an Anglo writer as a Chicano, as occurred in 1983 with Danny Santiago's *Famous All Over Town*. Rather, Cisneros' text is likely to continue to be excluded from the canon because it "speaks another language altogether," one to which the critics of the literary establishment "remain blind."

Besides the double marginalization that stems from gender and ethnicity, Cisneros transgresses the dominant discourse of canonical standards ideologically and linguistically. In bold contrast to the individualistic introspection of many canonical texts, Cisneros writes a modified autobiographical novel, or *Bildungsroman*, that roots the individual self in the broader socio-political reality of the Chicano community. As we will see, the story of individual development is oriented outwardly here, away from the bourgeois individualism of many standard texts. Cisneros' language also contributes to the text's otherness. In opposition to the complex, hermetic language of many canonical works, *The House on Mango Street* recuperates the simplicity of children's speech, paralleling the autobiographical protagonist's chronological age in the book. Although making the text accessible to people with a wider range of reading abilities, such simple and well-crafted prose is not currently in canonical vogue. . . .

On the surface the compelling desire for a house of one's own appears individualistic rather than community oriented, but Cisneros socializes the motif of the house, showing it to be a basic human need left unsatisfied for many of the minority population under capitalism. It is precisely the lack of housing stability that motivates the image's centrality in works by writers like Cisneros and Rivera. For the migrant worker who has moved continuously because of job exigencies and who, like many others in the Chicano community, has been deprived of an adequate place to live because of the inequities of income distribution in U.S. society, the desire for a house is not a sign of individualistic acquisitiveness but rather represents the satisfaction of a basic human need. . . .

Cisneros has socialized the motif of a house of one's own by showing its motivating roots to be the inadequate housing conditions in which she and others in her community lived. We learn that Esperanza, the protagonist Cisneros creates, was subjected to humiliation by her teachers because of her family's living conditions. *"You live there?"* a nun from her school had remarked when seeing Esperanza playing in front of the flat on Loomis. *"There.* I had to look where she pointed—the third floor, the paint peeling, wooden bars Papa had nailed on the windows so we wouldn't fall out. *You live there?* The way she said it made me feel like nothing. . . ." Later, after the move to the house on Mango Street that is better but still unsatisfactory, the Sister Superior at her school responds to Esperanza's request to eat lunch in the cafeteria rather than returning home by apparently humiliating the child deliberately: "You don't live far, she says . . . I bet I can see your house from my window. Which one? . . . That one? she said pointing to a row of ugly 3-flats, the ones even the raggedy men are ashamed to go into. Yes, I nodded even though I knew that wasn't my house and started to cry. . . ." The Sister Superior is revealing her own prejudices; in effect, she is telling the child, "All you Mexicans must live in such buildings." It is in response to humiliations such as these that the autobiographical protagonist expresses her need for a house of her own. Rather than the mere desire to possess private property, Esperanza's wish for a house represents a positive objectification of the self, the chance to redress humiliation and establish a dignified sense of her own personhood.

Cisneros links this positive objectification that a house of one's own can provide to the process of artistic creation.

Early on, the protagonist remarks that the dream of a white house "with trees around it, a great big yard and grass growing without a fence" structured the bedtime stories her mother told them. This early connection of the ideal house to fiction is developed throughout the collection, especially in the final two stories. In "A House of My Own," the protagonist remarks that the desired house would contain "my books and stories" and that such a house is as necessary to the writing process as paper: "Only a house quiet as snow, a space for myself to go, clean as paper before the poem." In "Mango Says Goodbye Sometimes," the Mango Street house, which falls short of the ideal dream house, becomes a symbol of the writer's attainment of her identity through artistic creation. Admitting that she both belonged and did not belong to the "*sad red house*" on Mango Street, the protagonist comes to terms with the ethnic consciousness that this house represents through the process of fictive creation: "I put it down on paper and then the ghost does not ache so much. I write it down and Mango says goodbye sometimes. She does not hold me with both arms. She sets me free." She is released materially to find a more suitable dwelling that will facilitate her writing; psychologically, she alleviates the ethnic anguish that she has heretofore attempted to repress. It is important, however, that she view her departure from the Mango Street house to enable her artistic production in social rather than isolationist terms: "They will know I have gone away to come back. For the ones I left behind. For the ones who cannot get out."

Unlike many introspective writers, then, Cisneros links both the process of artistic creation and the dream of a house that will enable this art to social rather than individualistic issues. In "Bums in the Attic," we learn that the protagonist dreams of a house on a hill similar to those where her father works as a gardener. Unlike those who own such houses now, Esperanza assures us that, were she to obtain such a house, she would not forget the people who live below: "One day I'll own my own house, but I won't forget who I am or where I came from. Passing bums will ask, Can I come in? I'll offer them the attic, ask them to stay, because I know how it is to be without a house." She conceives of a house as communal rather than private property; such sharing runs counter to the dominant ideological discourse that strongly affects consciousness in capitalists societies. Cisneros' social motifs undermine rather than support the widespread messages of individualized consumption that facilitate sales of goods and services under consumer capitalism. . . .

The majority of stories in *The House on Mango Street* . . . face important social issues head-on. The volume's simple, poetic language, with its insistence that the individual develops within a social community rather than in isolation, distances it from many accepted canonical texts.[6] Its deceptively simple, childlike prose and its emphasis on the unromanticized, non-mainstream issues of patriarchal violence and ethnic poverty, however, should serve precisely to accord it canonical status. We must work toward a broader understanding among literary critics of the importance of such issues to art in order to attain a richer, more diverse canon and to avoid the undervaluation and oversight of such valuable texts as *The House on Mango Street*.

Notes

1. Terry Eagleton, *Literary Theory: An Introduction* (Minneapolis: University of Minnesota Press, 1983), 201 and passim.

2. Sandra Cisneros, *The House on Mango Street* (Houston: Arte Público Press, 1985). Subsequent references will be to this edition and will appear in the text. For the figures on the press run see Pedro Gutiérrez-Revuelta, "Género e ideología en el libro de Sandra Cisneros: *The House on Mango Street*," *Crítica* 1, no. 3 (1986): 48–59.

3. Gutiérrez-Revuelta, "Género e ideología," 48. This critic also cites nine articles that have appeared to date on Cisneros' text. They consist primarily of reviews in Texas newspapers and articles in Chicano journals. See also Erlinda González-Berry and Tey Diana Rebolledo "Growing up Chicano: Tomás Rivera and Sandra Cisneros," *Revista Chicano–Riqueña* 13 (1985): 109–19.

6. Other critics have argued that Esperanza's departure from Mango Street is individualistic and escapist, and that the desire for a house of her own away from the barrio represents a belief in the American Dream. See Gutiérrez-Revuelta, "Género e ideología," 52–55 and Juan Rodríguez, "The House on Mango Street by Sandra Cisneros," *Austin Chronicle*, 10 Aug. 1984 (cited in Gutiérrez-Revuelta, p. 52). I find that

the text itself supports the opposite view, as does the author's choice of employment. Cisneros has returned to a Chicago barrio, teaching creative writing at an alternative high school for drop-outs. See "About Sandra Cisneros," *The House on Mango Street*, 103.

ANNIE O. EYSTUROY ON HOUSE SYMBOLISM IN *THE HOUSE ON MANGO STREET*

As the title indicates, both "the house" and "Mango Street" are central symbols throughout the novel. Mango Street and the house Esperanza lives in constitute her world, the world she has to come to grips with as she grows up. It is her response to this particular environment, the interplay between psychological and social forces, that determines the direction of her *Bildungs* process. It is through her dialectical relationship to the house—in other words, the private sphere, the family, the collective memory—as well as to Mango Street—that is, the social sphere, the larger Hispanic community—that the narrating "I" comes to an understanding of her own individual self. Esperanza's world on Mango Street is a world unto its own, an Hispanic barrio of a large American city, yet unspecified in respect to its exact geographical and historical setting, a symbolic "microcosm for the larger world" (Gonzáles-Berry and Rebolledo, 114) that lends a universal quality to this Chicana *Bildungsroman*.

It is significant that the initial word in this Chicana quest novel is "We": "We didn't always live on Mango Street" (7). Esperanza recalls her family history of moving from one dilapidated house to another until they finally move into their own house on Mango Street, yet the house is not what the family had hoped for: "The house on Mango Street is ours. . . . But even so, it's not the house we'd thought we'd get" (7). Esperanza's sense of self is here firmly lodged within the collective identity of her family. It is, however, in this initial story, homonymous with the novel itself, that the narrating "I" becomes aware of her own subjective perceptions as she begins to differentiate between family dreams and social realities and becomes conscious of her parents' inability to fulfill their promises of the perfect house. "They always told us that one day we would move into a house, a real house" (7). The "real house" Esperanza expected would be "like the houses on TV":

> Our house would be white with trees around it, a great big yard and grass growing without a fence. This was the house Papa talked about when he held a lottery ticket and this was the house Mama dreamed up in the stories she told us before we went to bed.
>
> But the house on Mango Street is not the way she told it at all. (8)

The house is just the opposite of what she had been told would be their house one day, a fact that stands in direct opposition to the words of her parents. This contrast between expectation and reality awakens her awareness of herself as a social being and provokes her own interpretations of the significance the house holds in her life.

Esperanza sees the house on Mango Street as a symbol of poverty that she associates with the humiliation she has felt in the past, living in similar places:

> Where do you live? she said.
> There, I said, pointing up to the third floor.
> You live *there*?
> *There*. I had to look to where she pointed—the third, the paint peeling, wooden bars Papa had nailed on the windows so we wouldn't fall out.
> You live *there*? The way she said it made me feel like nothing. *There*. I lived *there*. I nodded. (8–9)

In another situation a teacher prejudicially assumes that Esperanza, because she is Chicana, lives in a building that "even the raggedy men are ashamed to go into" (43), thus automatically identifying her with the poverty and degradation the house represents. Made to feel ashamed of living in houses other people show obvious contempt for, thus ashamed of "her entire social and subject position" (Saldívar, 1990, 182), Esperanza sees the house as a symbol of the shame that threatens her own self-perception. To Esperanza the house on Mango Street is an emblem of the oppressive socioeconomic situation that circumscribes her life and is the source of her feelings of alienation. It is this alienation that becomes a catalyst for her desire to distance herself from this "sad red house" (101) she does not want to belong to.

This psychological rejection of the house on Mango Street is further underscored by her own description of the house as narrow and confining, where even the windows appear to be "holding their breath" (8), a description that shows an almost claustrophobic reaction to her parents' house. According to Cirlot, breathing is a process whereby one assimilates spiritual power. Esperanza's perception of the house as not breathing is indicative of the spiritual suffocation the house represents. This depiction of the house is, as Julián Olivares points out, "a metonymical description and presentation of the self" (162), a self that feels constrained as well as ashamed when identified with a house that represents only confinement and therefore knows that she needs another house, one that would liberate her from the oppression of her present situation:

> I knew then I had to have a house. A real house. One I could point to. But this isn't it. The house on Mango Street isn't it. For the time being, Mama said. Temporary, said Papa. But I know how these things go. (9)

The last phrase, "But I know . . . ," indicates the emerging consciousness of the protagonist, that her passage from childhood innocence to knowledge has begun, a development that marks the beginning of her *Bildungs* process. Through her own interpretative agency she now knows that she cannot rely on what her parents tell her and that they will not be able to provide her with the house that she needs. Although at this point she imagines a "real house" to be something like the Dick and Jane reader's version of an American home, the importance of the house lies not so much in its physical features as in its symbolic value in a sociocultural context. . . .

Like the house, Mango Street is the physical and psychological marker of an oppressive socioeconomic situation that makes Esperanza conscious of her own status in a socioeconomic hierarchy: "The neighborhood is getting bad," she says, and this is why people have to move "a little farther away every time people like us keep moving in" (15). Much as with the house, a negative analogy is established between Esperanza and her barrio; she lives there and therefore the neighborhood is "getting bad," the narrating "I" again being defined by her external, socioeconomic circumstances:

> Those who don't know any better come into our neighborhood scared. They think we're dangerous. They think we will attack them with shiny knives. They are stupid people who are lost and got here by mistake. (29)

The implications of being defined by a poor, deteriorating neighborhood and prejudicial stereotypes make Esperanza conscious of the particular socioeconomic conditions that circumscribe her life and trap her in a marginalized world of "too much sadness and not enough sky" (33).

Despite the cumulative threat the house and Mango Street present to her sense of self, however, she begins to imagine herself beyond Mango Street, determined to "make the best of it" (33). Estranged by the social implications of living in this environment, Esperanza disavows her relationship to Mango Street—"I don't ever want to come from here" (99)—identifying herself with the only piece of nature present in the barrio, four trees "who do not belong here but are here":

> Their strength is secret. . . . When I am a tiny thing against so many bricks, then it is I look at trees. When there is nothing left to look at on this street. Four who grew despite concrete. Four who reach and do not forget to reach. (71)

This identification with a small piece of nature in this urban environment exemplifies the primacy of nature in female development, when the adolescent feels "a sense of oneness with cosmos" (Pratt, 1981, 17) as an alternative to her alienation from an oppressive environment. In her longing to escape her present circumstances, Esperanza sees the trees as role models for her own liberation: they grow "despite concrete," thus symbolizing Esperanza's own struggle to grow in a hostile environment, her desire to reach beyond the concrete, beyond class and race boundaries, for self-definition.

MYRNA-YAMIL GONZÁLES ON FEMALE VOICES OF INFLUENCE

In *Mango Street* Cisneros creates a protagonist that is a storyteller and a mythmaker who draws upon old tales and new experiences to create an impressionistic poetics of a culturally diverse Chicago neighborhood; the structure of the narrative suggests the influence of oral traditions and the blending of cultural identities (March 183). The young narrator has internalized the worldview and experiences of her parents, her friends, and the society of which she is a part as she strives to locate her identity. . . .

Esperanza's name, which means "hope" in Spanish, can also mean a wait (*espera*). She has inherited her great-grandmother's name but must deconstruct it; Esperanza's great-grandmother is a subjugated Mexican woman who had been taken away from her family by force. She therefore embodies a submissive female model that the young Esperanza must reject. But Esperanza would like to go even farther: she would change her name completely to redirect her life away from a possible repetition of her ancestor's sad history. "I would like to baptize myself under a new name, a name like the real me, the one nobody sees. Esperanza as Lisandra or Maritza or Zeze the X. Yes. Something like Zeze the X will do" (11). . . .

Women's lives are circumscribed by cultural values and norms that dictate their behavior and roles; female authors often suggest new roles or imbue existing models with more accessible and more affirming traits and characteristics. Among Chicana writers, many have been inspired by the representation of power and control of such Aztec goddesses as Coatlicue, and the nurturing tradition of the Christian Virgin of Guadalupe, the patron saint of Mexico. The traditional figure of the *curandera/bruja* or healer/witch has also emerged as a powerful female symbol. The *curandera* has two attributes: a positive one as a healer and a negative one as a *bruja* or witch/seer. The *curandera* possesses intuitive and cognitive skills; her connection to and interrelation with the natural world is part of her ancient knowledge. The fact that the curandera has emerged as a powerful figure in the writing of both women and men demonstrates not only her enduring representational qualities as myth and symbol but also the close identification of the culture with her mystic and spiritual qualities (Rebolledo 83–84). Cisneros' *curanderas* in *Mango Street* are of the affirming variety.

In "The Three Sisters," for example, Esperanza comes in contact with *curanderas* on two different occasions. Her first experience is with Elenita, the seer first mentioned in "Elenita, Cards, Palm, Water." Elenita's deeds are performed in the kitchen, the section of the house containing all the implements required for her craft. Among the tasks required of Esperanza is to fill a cup with water in order to attempt to see what Elenita perceives, particularly peoples' faces, but Esperanza sees nothing. Elenita then proceeds to read the tarot cards: "now my fortune begins. My whole life on that kitchen table: past, present and future" (63). Finally Elenita reads her palms, where she sees jealousy, sorrow, a pillar of bees, and a "mattress of luxury" (63). Esperanza wants to know only about a house, but the only home Elenita sees is in the heart: "a new house, a house made of heart. I'll light a candle for you. Thank you and goodbye and be careful of the evil eye" (64). Esperanza pays her five dollars and leaves, left puzzled by the oracle.

Esperanza then encounters three mysterious sisters, describing them as "one with laughter like tin and one with eyes of a cat and one with hands like porcelain. . . . They had the power and could sense what was what" (103–4). One of them, "the old blue-veined" sister, asks her name. When Esperanza replies, she is told it is a good name. The one with cat eyes tells the others to look at Esperanza's hands, and they inform her that she is special and foretell a future in which she will go very far. . . .

For Tey Diana Rebolledo, the *curandera* is a compelling figure in Chicano literature precisely because she is a woman who has control over her own life and destiny as well as that of others. The *curandera* has a special relationship to the earth and nature—she understands the cycles of creation, development, and destruction, unifying the past, present, and future. Incorporating intuition and rationality, the *curandera* bends or harnesses power; she takes an active role in her environment. She listens carefully and thus understands collective as well as individual psychology embedded in ethnic beliefs and practices and can be perceived as a cultural psychologist or psychiatrist. Individual human behavior is always weighed against communal good. The *curandera* intimately understands community (Rebolledo 87–88). . . .

Mujeres andariegas (wandering women) and *mujeres callejeras* (street women) are terms that imply both restlessness and wickedness. These are women who do not stay at home tending to their husbands, children, and parents. Unbound by socially construed morals or cultural practices, they must therefore be, by implication, wicked: *putas*, or loose women. The negative cultural stereotypes placed on *mujeres andariegas* result from a patriarchal culture that wills women to be passive, self-denying, and nurturing.

Another perspective, however, is to view these literary and real women as *mujeres de fuerza*—strong, independent women, who are self-sufficient; they thrive and prosper in spite of the possible consequences of their actions (Rebolledo 183). The cultural ideal of the self-sacrificing girl who stays at home and lets others control her body—the Virgin of Guadalupe ideal—and its opposite, the woman who controls her own sexuality and destiny—the powerful pre-Columbian Aztec goddess ideal—are both elements of the Chicana cultural and literary heritage. So too are the women who dare to speak out on public issues, often defined as troublemakers for actively seeking change and seeking justice, a common theme throughout Chicana literature (Rebolledo 189–90). The "bad girl" image, another common theme, is associated with the female awareness of sexuality, the desire to understand the erotic self and sensual capabilities that clash with the cultural norms of a strong traditional family, and the limitations imposed by the Church and a male-oriented society (Rebolledo 192).

In *Mango Street*, Esperanza risks censure by defying convention. "I have begun my own quiet war. Simple. Sure. I am one who leaves the table like a man, without putting back the chair or picking up the plate" (89). In her fantasy, when she is grown, she will be like the woman who is "beautiful and cruel . . . the one who drives men crazy and laughs at them all the way. Her power is her own. She will not give it away" (89). This, however, is an idealized desire; it ignores the possibility that being wicked or defiant does not exempt women from suffering. . . .

In many ways Cisneros' work reflects the concern of contemporary Chicana feminism which combines the question of gender and sexuality with issues of race, culture, and class. . . . [P]erhaps the most important principle of Chicana feminist criticism is the realization that the Chicana's experience as a woman is inextricable from her experience as a member of an oppressed working-class racial minority and an ethnic subculture. . . . The fact that Chicanas tell stories about themselves and other Chicanas/Latinas challenges the dominant male concepts of cultural ownership and literary authority and rejects the dominant culture's definition of what a Chicana is. In writing, they refuse the objectification imposed by gender roles and racial and economic limitations. The Chicana writer finds that the self she seeks to define is not an individual self but a collective one. In other words, the power, the permission, the authority to tell stories about herself and other Chicanas come from her cultural, racial/ethnic, and linguistic community, a community with a literary tradition.

The Chicana writer derives literary authority from the oral tradition of her community, which in turn empowers her to commit her stories to writing (734). . . .

In *The House on Mango Street*, therefore, Sandra Cisneros presents a diversity of female voices from the marginalized perspective of the Chicana/Latina experience. Her house and its environment symbolize women's spaces and afford the protagonist an identity with her immediate and extended barrio family. Ultimately, however, Esperanza's true identity and freedom will be found in her writing; there she discovers the recipe for achieving her goals while never forgetting her origins. Her writing helps her—and us—make sense of the world around her and the women who are a part of that world. It is offered to "the ones I left behind . . . the ones who cannot out" (110) and it offers the possibility that a woman can achieve anything in life if she can locate the strength and courage to leave confining situations and discover who she truly is.

Criticism and Further Reading

Castillo, Debra A. "Toward a Latin American Feminist Literary Practice." In *Talking Back: Toward a Latin American Feminist Literary Theory Criticism*, ed. Debra A. Castillo. Ithaca: Cornell University Press, 1992, 1–70.

Cisneros, Sandra. *The House on Mango Street*. New York: Vintage Contemporaries, 1991. All references in the text are to this edition.

Corson, Nancy Carter. "Claiming the Bittersweet Matrix: Alice Walker, Sandra Cisneros, and Adrienne Rich." *Critique: Studies in Modern Fiction* 35, no. 4 (Summer 1994): 195–204.

Doyle, Jacqueline. "More Room of Her Own: Sandra Cisneros's *The House on Mango Street*." *MELUS* 19, no. 4 (Winter 1994): 5–35. This analysis explores the similarities, connections, and transformations of *A Room of One's Own* by Virginia Woolf and *The House on Mango Street*.

Gutiérrez-Jones, Leslie S. "Different Voices: The Re-Bildung of the Barrio in Sandra Cisneros's *The House on Mango Street*." In *Anxious Power: Reading, Writing, and Ambivalence in Narrative by Women*, eds. Carol J. Singley and Susan Elizabeth Sweeney. Albany: State University of New York Press, 1993, 295–312.

Jussawalla, Feroza, and Reed Way Dasenbrock. "Sandra Cisneros." In *Interviews with Writers of the Post-Colonial World*, eds. Feroza Jussawalla and Reed Way Dasenbrock. Jackson: University Press of Mississippi, 1992, 286–306.

March, Jayne E. "Difference, Identity, and Sandra Cisneros' *The House on Mango Street*." *Hungarian Journal of English and American Studies* 2, no. 1 (1996): 173–87.

Olivares, Julian. "Entering the House on Mango Street." In *Teaching American Ethnic Literatures: Nineteen Essays*, eds. John R. Maitino and David R. Peck. Albuquerque: University of New Mexico Press, 1996, 209–35. An excellent essay that compares *Mango Street* with . . . *y no se lo tragó la tierra* by Tomás Rivera and explores the literary tradition of Chicanas. Olivares suggests topics for teaching the work.

———. "Sandra Cisneros' *The House on Mango Street* and the Poetics of Space." In *Beyond Stereotypes: The Critical Analysis of Chicana Literature*, ed. María Herrera-Sobek. Binghamton, N.Y.: Bilingual Press, 1985, 160–70.

Rebolledo, Tey Diana. *Women Singing in the Snow*. Tucson: University of Arizona Press, 1995.

Saldívar-Hull, Sonia. "Mujeres en lucha: Women in Struggle in Sandra Cisneros's *The House on Mango Street*." In *Feminism on the Border: From Gender Politics to Geopolitics*. Ph.D. diss., University of Texas at Austin, 1990, 84–127.

Sloboda, Nicholas. "A Home in the Heart: Sandra Cisneros's *The House on Mango Street*." *Aztlán* 22 (Fall 1997): 89–106.

Yarbro-Bejarano, Yvonne. "Chicana Literature from a Chicana Feminist Perspective." In *Feminisms: An Anthology of Literary Theory and Criticism*, eds. Robyn R. Warhol and Diane Price Herndl. New Brunswick, N.J.: Rutgers University Press, 1993, 732–37.

DEBORAH L. MADSEN ON SANDRA CISNEROS AND THE WRITING LIFE

Cisneros's work is characterized by the celebratory breaking of sexual taboos and trespassing across the restrictions that limit the lives and experiences of Chicanas. These themes of trespass, transgression, and joyful abandon feature prominently in her poetry. The narrative techniques of her fiction demonstrate daring technical innovations, especially in her bold experimentation with literary voice and her development of a hybrid form that weaves poetry into prose to create a dense and evocative linguistic texture of symbolism and imagery that is both technically and aesthetically accomplished. . . .

Cisneros describes writing as something she has done all her life from the time when, as a young girl, she began writing in spiral notebooks poems that only her mother read. Her first published book, *Bad Boys*, appeared as the Chicano Chapbook No. 8 (1980). Her novel *The House on Mango Street* was published by a small regional press in 1984 and the following year was awarded the Before Columbus Foundation's American Book Award. The novel draws heavily upon childhood memories and an unadorned childlike style of expression to depict life in the Chicano community. Issues of racial and sexual oppression, poverty, and violence are explored in a sequence of interconnected vignettes that together form a modified autobiographical structure. *Woman Hollering Creek and Other Stories* continues the exploration of ethnic identity within the patriarchal context of Chicano culture. The stories in this volume offer snapshots of Mexican American life: sights and smells recalled in childish memories, stories told by witches who see all of Chicano history from past to future, the hopes and aspirations of grandparents and grandchildren, friends and neighbors, Mexican movies, and "Merican" tourists. Her first volume of poetry, *My Wicked, Wicked Ways*, is described by Cherríe Moraga as "a kind of international graffiti, where the poet—bold and insistent—puts her mark on those travelled places on the map and in the heart."[3] *Loose Woman* similarly invokes the cultural and the emotional in an intoxicating sequence of outrageously confessional moments. Cisneros has also published essays on writing and her role as a writer, most notably the selections titled "From a Writer's Notebook. Ghosts and Voices: Writing from Obsession" and "Notes to a Young(er) Writer," both of which appeared in the *Americas Review* (1987). Her books have been translated into ten languages.

In Cisneros's work the effort to negotiate a cross-cultural identity is complicated by the need to challenge the deeply rooted patriarchal values of both Mexican and American cultures. Cisneros writes, "There's always this balancing act, we've got to define what we think is fine for ourselves instead of what our culture says."[4] Chicana feminism has arisen largely from this need to contest the feminine stereotypes that define machismo, while at the same time identifying and working against the shared class and racial oppression that all Chicanos/as—men, women and children—experience. To adopt models of femininity that are thought of as Anglo is, as Cisneros describes, to be told you're a traitor to your culture. And it's a horrible life to live. We're always straddling two countries, and we're always living in that kind of schizophrenia that I call, being a Mexican woman living in an American society, but not belonging to either culture. In some sense we're not Mexican and in some sense we're not American.[5]

Patriarchal definitions of feminine subjectivity, some Anglo but mostly Mexican, affect all of Cisneros's characters by creating the medium in which they live. The protagonist of *The House on Mango Street*, the girl Esperanza, compares herself with her great-grandmother with whom she shares her name and the coincidence of being born in the Chinese year of the horse, which is supposed to be bad luck if you're born female— but I think this is a Chinese lie because the Chinese, like the Mexicans, don't like their women strong.[6] This fiery ancestor, "a wild horse of a woman, so wild she wouldn't marry" (*Mango Street*, 11), is forcibly taken by Esperanza's great-grandfather, and her spirit broken, she lived out her days staring from her window. The narrator remarks, "I have inherited her name, but I don't want to inherit her place by the window" (11). This woman is the first of many Esperanza encounters who are broken in body and spirit by the patriarchal society that defines the terms by which they live.

The primary effect of these prescriptive definitions is the experience of the self as marginal, as failing to belong in the culture in which one lives. Cisneros challenges marginality but in subtle ways and using the weapons at her disposal as an artist: imagery, symbolism, forms of narrative connectivity that are at odds with rational, discursive logic. Like so many Chicana writers, Sandra Cisneros rejects the logic of the patriarchy in favor of more provisional, personal, emotional, and intuitive forms of narrative. She creates stories, not explanations or analyses or arguments. The stories that comprise *The House on Mango Street* are linked according to a loose and associative logic. In this way the fragmented structure of the text embodies a quest for freedom, a genuine liberation that resolves rather than escapes the conflicts faced by the Chicana subject. María Elena de Valdés describes how Cisneros's narrative technique relates to the theme of feminist resistance: "The open-ended reflections are the narrator's search for an answer to the enigma: how can she be free of Mango Street and the house that is not hers and yet belong as she must to that house and that street. The open-ended entries come together only slowly as the tapestry takes shape, for each of the closed figures are also threads of the larger background figure which is the narrator herself."[7] The threads with which the story is then woven are the complex image patterns Cisneros gradually develops and the imagistic connections she builds among the vignettes. The first story, which describes the houses in which Esperanza has lived, ends with her father's promise that their cramped and shabby house is temporary. The next story, "Hairs," begins with a description of her father's hair and goes on to contrast it with her mother's. The contrast between mother and father is continued and generalized in the third story, "Boys and Girls," which ends with Esperanza's hope that she will one day have the best friend for whom she yearns. The fourth story concerns the meaning of Esperanza's name, "Hope." In this way Cisneros creates vignettes that are self-contained, autonomous, yet link together in an emotionally logical fashion and build to create a picture of life in the barrio, seen through the experiences of the young Esperanza and her developing consciousness of herself as an artist. . . .

Power is a word that recurs constantly when describing Sandra Cisneros's writing. She has described the Chicana writer as someone who is necessarily an obsessive. By virtue of who she is and the circumstances of her birth, the Chicana writer has no leisure to pursue the aesthetic just for its own sake. She is motivated not so much by inspiration but by the need to articulate pressing issues and to give expression to the ghosts that haunt her.[26] "Night Madness Poem" describes this compulsion to seek relief in the crafting of words. The poem that seeks expression is likened to "A pea under twenty eiderdowns. / A sadness in my heart like stone" (*Loose Woman*, 49, 2.3–4). As the poem continues, we realize that the words Cisneros wants to speak are to the absent lover she cannot telephone, but these are also the words of her poetry. Frustrated love and frustrated writing merge and are confused, so the poem ends with a challenge: "Choose your weapon. / Mine— the telephone, my tongue" (2.30–31). . . .

The 1992 preface to the reprinted collection . . . introduces the primary themes: the difficult choice to become a writer, the transgression of family and cultural expectation: "A woman like me / whose choice was rolling pin or factory / An absurd vice, this wicked wanton / writer's life" (*Wicked Ways*, x). The poem "His Story" develops this theme by presenting the father's view of his nonconformist daughter. He searches among family precedents for women who have trespassed across the borders of approved feminine behavior, trying to find an explanation for his sorrow. The poem concludes with the poet's reflection on her father's explorations: "An unlucky fate is mine / to be born woman in a family of men"; and her father's lament: "Six sons, my father groans, / all home. / And one female, / gone" (*Wicked Ways*, 38–39, 2.33–34, 35–38). The poems that follow this preface are then presented as the offspring of her union with the poetic muse: a brood of "colicky kids / who fussed and kept / me up the wicked nights" (*Wicked Ways*, xii). And in poems such as "The Poet Reflects on Her Solitary Fate," Cisneros describes the compulsion to write, the need to express her creativity: "The house is cold. / There is nothing on TV. / She must write poems" (*Wicked Ways*, 37, 2.13–15).

Though this poem, like all of Cisneros's work, is intensely personal she has discovered how to uncover the subtle and intricate web of connections that bind the personal with the cultural. Cisneros begins with personal experiences, feelings, and thoughts and suggests the complex ways in which these attributes of the private self have been shaped, prescribed, and monitored by cultural, racial, political, and economic forces. Her sense of responsibility as a writer is conceived in terms of these social and cultural influences. She explains that she is the first woman in her family to assume a public voice through writing, to take upon herself the power to speak and find that she is heard.[28] This privilege brings with it a responsibility to witness the lives and to register the worlds of those who remain invisible: the powerless, the silent. Cisneros tells of how she admires the poetry of Emily Dickinson and what she took to be Dickinson's ability to live both domestic and artistic lives simultaneously. Then Cisneros discovered Dickinson's housekeeper, the woman who performed the routine chores to keep the household running, freeing Dickinson to pursue her intellectual work. Cisneros describes how Emily Dickinson's housekeeper helped her to recognize the enormous contribution her own mother made to enable the young Sandra to read and write when instead she should have been washing dishes.[29]

In a sense, then, Cisneros's work is dedicated to her mother and to Emily Dickinson's housekeeper, the women who are forgotten but who made possible the lives of other literary women. In her essay "Cactus Flowers" Cisneros describes the courage it takes to define oneself as a Chicana writer: "To admit you are a writer takes a great deal of audacity. To admit you are a feminist takes even greater courage. It is admirable then when Chicana writers elect to redefine and reinvent themselves through their writing."[30] To be a writer is, for Sandra Cisneros, to have the opportunity to do something for the silenced women and for all women by inventing new paradigms, by defining new Chicana voices, and by living as a liberated feminine subject of the story she has written for herself.

Notes

3. Cherríe Moraga, jacket blurb, Sandra Cisneros, *My Wicked, Wicked Ways* (1987); rpt. (New York: Alfred K. Knopf, 1995).

4. Aranda, "Interview," 66.

5. Ibid.

6. Sandra Cisneros, *The House on Mango Street* (1984); rpt. (London: Bloomsbury, 1992), 10. Future page references are given in the text.

7. María Elena de Valdés, "The Critical Reception of Sandra Cisneros's *The House on Mango Street*, in *Gender, Self, and Society Proceedings of IV International Conference on the Hispanic Cultures of the United States*, ed. Renate von Bardelben (Frankfurt, Germany: Peter Lang, 1993), 293.

26. See Cisneros, "Ghosts and Voices," 73.

28. See Sandra Cisneros, "Notes to a Young(er) Writer," *Americas Review* 15 (Spring 1987): 76.

29. Ibid., 75.

30. Cisneros, "Cactus Flowers," 79.

Patsy J. Daniels on Transforming the World with Words

Latina literature in the United States is attaining status in the academy as a part of American literature. Latina writers, too, much like the Asian American writers and the African American writers, are mining their ancestral traditions, exposing oppression, and rewriting history from their own point of view. They, too, are gaining a voice in America as the result of straddling boundaries and synthesizing cultures. The two writers whose works are discussed here, Sandra Cisneros and Ana Castillo, consider themselves to be part of a subgroup of Latinas that they call Chicanas, a label which came about as the result of political struggles. They speak from their own experience, their own reality, which is the reality of other American women of Latin background, but by no means of all. These two authors invent hybrid literary genres and hybrid language, and their protagonists use the power of the word to provide a space from which to speak to the world. And speak they do. Sandra Cisneros, in *The House on Mango Street*, protests against racism and classism, but also against the patriarchy's control of women and their sexuality. Ana Castillo has been known as a "protest poet." In her novel *So Far From God* can be found protests against all of the elements of the system of colonization: the corporations, the patriarchy of the church, and the government. But both writers do more than simply protest; they suggest a way to transform the world through the use of words. . . .

Cisneros makes clear the need for a change in society. As Cisneros's adolescent protagonist Esperanza grows up, she learns that there is a difference between appearance and reality.

The patriarchal system she and her community live under covers up the truth and romanticizes women's roles so that the women will accept their roles as either whores or wives. For example, the system romanticizes sex, but Esperanza finds out through her violent and humiliating initiation to sexual intercourse that there is nothing romantic about sex. Esperanza blames her rude awakening not only on her individual friend Sally, who knows about sex already and who has failed to either inform or rescue her, but also the whole system: "Sally, you lied. It wasn't what you said at all. . . . The way they said it, the way it's supposed to be, all the storybooks and movies, why did you lie to me?" (Cisneros 99). Later, Esperanza continues her diatribe: "I waited my whole life. You're a liar. They all lied. All the books and magazines, everything that told it wrong" (100). Sally isn't there to save Esperanza the way Esperanza has attempted to save Sally when Sally disappears with Tito and his buddies. Then Esperanza excitedly runs to Tito's mother for help, but the mother has a calm reaction: "Those kids, she said, not looking up from her ironing. . . . What do you want me to do, she said, call the cops? And kept on ironing" (97). Tito's mother has accepted women's place in a male-centered society many years before. But Sally has also accepted the same role; Sally doesn't want to be saved. Sally probably believes that Esperanza doesn't really want to be rescued either.

In addition, the women are taught that there is romantic love and a happily-ever-after life for them when they marry, but they soon find out the truth about their role in marriage and about the drudgery, the violence, and the loneliness that they must endure. Esperanza is gradually coming to the realization that "boys make the rules" and decides to break their rules by leaving her dishes on the table "like a man" (Cisneros 89). Dianne Klein looks at Esperanza's growing awareness as a typical coming-of-age story, but with a twist. She writes,

> Esperanza's rites of passage speak not through myth and dreams, but through the political realities of Mango Street. She faces pain and experiences violence in a very different way. Her major loss of innocence has to do with gender

and with being sexually appropriated by men. . . . Perhaps Esperanza's "descent into darkness" occurs in the story "Red Clowns." Unlike the traditional bildungsroman, the knowledge with which she emerges is not that of regeneration, but of painful knowledge, the knowledge of betrayal and physical violation. . . . [T]hrough books and magazines and the talk of women she has been led to believe the myth of romantic love. (25)

Klein writes that Maria Herrera-Sobek calls "The Red Clowns" a "'diatribe' that is directed not only at Sally, 'but at the community of women in a conspiracy of silence . . . silence in not denouncing the "real" facts of life about sex and its negative aspects in violent sexual encounters, and *complicity* in romanticizing and idealizing unrealistic sexual relations'" (qtd. in Klein 25).

Other lies that men use to keep women in their place include the "imaginary" mice that Alicia sees. Her father tells her that she does not really see mice in the kitchen as she studies at night, that it is "all in her head," but Alicia knows they are real; she trusts her own experience and sees through her father's lies. That's why she is taking steps to leave her father's house. Even though she is afraid of her father, she studies and endures hardships to prepare herself for another life. Like Joyce's Eveline in *Dubliners*, Alicia has inherited her dead mother's responsibilities toward her father. She is able to fulfill these responsibilities in addition to doing her school work; unlike Eveline, she is able to take positive action to improve her situation in life. Alicia sees through her father's attempts to cover up reality.

But the biggest difference between appearance and reality is the one between Esperanza's dream house and the real house on Mango Street. Even though her parents have described the dream house, they have been able to provide only the house on Mango Street, which falls far short of the dream house, just as marriage falls short of its romantic ideal. Esperanza equates the house with herself; it is the outward representation of her identity. She knows that she does not belong to such a substandard house, which has been built and left behind by

Cathy's white family as they move up on the socio-economic ladder. Esperanza does not want to accept this house as her station in life. Instead, she intends to be like the house of her dreams. She already knows that she is, on the inside, but no one else can tell because all they can see is the outside, where she doesn't fit into the hegemonic cultural trappings.

Esperanza and her friends and neighbors make several attempts to fit into the dominant society that they live in, but each time they pay a heavy price. When the children attempt to imitate Tarzan, a cultural icon, they jump from a tree and Meme breaks both arms. The moral of this story is that it is painful to try to emulate Hollywood images; they are not reality. Louie's "other cousin" also pays a heavy price for his joyride in a Cadillac. He takes the children for a ride, and for a while they enjoy the cultural trappings of capitalism, but it quickly ends. The price Louie's other cousin pays is a beating from the police when they arrest him. Esperanza herself ends up paying heavily for her attempt to be like the "others." She wants to eat her lunch at school like the children do whose mothers are not at home at lunchtime, but she leaves herself open to humiliation as the nun questions why Esperanza does not eat at her home, which is close by. When the nun points out a house even worse than the one Esperanza lives in and makes Esperanza claim it, Esperanza realizes that she must live farther away if she wants to change her situation. She must live farther away in order to eat lunch at school; she must live farther away in order to improve her opportunities. For a real change in her life, it is not enough to break the rules at home; at home she must still choose between a father and a husband. And the nun has demonstrated that she must live farther away.

Sally, too, pays dearly for her freedom from her father. She marries before eighth grade and has material things like Sofia's daughter Fe in Castillo's novel, but finds, like Fe, that the price is steep. Her husband sometimes gives her money, but he commits violence against her, won't let her talk on the phone or look out the window, and won't allow her friends to visit when he is at home. Sally has discovered the reality beneath the fantasy. When the young girls have their high-heel adventure, they, too, pay the price for looking "beautiful." They discover that a pillar of the community, the grocer, will threaten them with the police to control them, that a boy will make cat-calls at them to exploit them, that other girls will actively ignore them to compete with them, and that a bum will attempt to entice them with money for "a kiss," representing either prostitution or marriage. This is the legacy that one of the mothers passes on to them when she hands them the bag of shoes to play with. She asks, "Do you want it?" as if the girls actually have a choice. When the girls have grown "tired of being beautiful" (Cisneros 42), Lucy's mother throws the shoes away, a sign that gender roles could change, that the girls could have more choices than their mothers have had. Esperanza's mother counsels her daughter, too, about staying in school, telling her not to be discouraged enough to quit school for a superficial reason the way the mother has done—because she was ashamed of her clothes. The idea is, of course, that Esperanza's mother could still have gained an education, even in poor clothing, that Esperanza can still grow up to become a writer in the Mango Street house, even if it is humble.

Esperanza realizes early on that boys and girls have separate worlds and that she has responsibilities to those who come after her as seen in the story "Boys & Girls." Her brothers refuse to acknowledge Esperanza and her sister Nenny outside of the house; the brothers have a separate life outside, and it is the "boys [who] invented the rules" (Cisneros 96). It is in this story, too, that Esperanza realizes that she can help her little sister. In other words, Esperanza has a responsibility not only to herself to grow individually, but also to those who come after her to help the community to grow collectively.

HELENA GRICE ON OPPOSITIONAL PAIRINGS IN THE NOVEL

The House on Mango Street is a coming-of-age narrative, which centres upon the life of Esperanza Cordero, who relates her story in the first person. . . . Perhaps as a result of its popularity on high school curricula, the text has sometimes been pigeonholed as an adolescent narrative, a view which is strengthened by the deceptively simple narrative structure and the prevailing adolescent viewpoint. However, this belies the sophistication of the vignette structure which enables the construction of an elaborate series of oppositional tropes and preoccupations, which surface repeatedly in the different stories. . . .

In common with other Chicana writers, Cisneros' exploration of different versions of femininity in the novel also provides a commentary upon and critique of wider historical Chicano myths and stereotypes of womanhood. Specifically, a dichotomy is constructed in the text between a '*virgen*' (virgin) and a '*puta*' (whore)—two archetypes which derive from two mythological figures in Chicano/a culture, la Malinche, and la Virgen de Guadalupe. La Malinche, also known as Doña Marina or Malintzin, was an aristocratic Aztec woman who was reputed to have betrayed her people by helping to ensure Hernán Cortés' conquest of the Aztec Empire at the beginning of the sixteenth century, and she also slept with him. A son resulted from this union, thus producing a 'mestizo' (mixed-race) child and subsequently a whole new hybrid race. Thus negatively iconised as a Chicana 'Eve', a *mujer mala* ('bad woman'), la Malinche burdens Chicana culture with a problematic legacy, as both Gloria Anzaldúa and Norma Alarcón have noted. (Alarcón describes la Malinche as 'a male myth' in her essay, 'Chicana's Feminist Literature', in *This Bridge Called My Back*, eds Cherríe Moraga and Gloria Anzaldúa, Kitchen Table: Women of Color Press, 1981, p. 184.) Equally problematic to Chicanas is the image and iconography of la Virgen de Guadalupe (the Virgin of Guadalupe). Gloria Anzaldúa argues that '*La Virgen de Guadalupe* is the single most potent religious, political and cultural image of the Chicano/*mexicano*' (*Borderlands/La Frontera*, p. 30). Anzaldúa further argues she is problematic for Chicanas because she 'has been used by the Church to mete out institutionalized oppression' and 'to make us docile and enduring' (p. 30). In fact, for Anzaldúa, la Malinche, la

Virgen de Guadalupe and la Llorona (the weeping woman), together work as a symbolic triptych: '*La gente Chicana tiene tres madres*. All three are mediators: *Guadalupe*, the virgin mother who has not abandoned us, *la chingada* (*Malinche*), the raped mother whom we have abandoned, and *la Llorona*, the mother who seeks her lost children and is a combination of the other two' (p. 30). Similarly, Norma Alarcón notes: 'Insofar as feminine symbolic figures are concerned, much of the Mexican/Chicano oral tradition as well as the intellectual are dominated by la Malinche/la Llorona and the Virgin of Guadalupe. . . . The Mexican/Chicano cultural tradition has tended to polarize the lives of women through these national [and nationalistic] symbols' ('Chicana's Feminist Literature', p. 189).

Cisneros manipulates these models of femininity for her own purposes. If female sexuality is often figured as a burden in the text, then it sometimes also offers a possible means of manipulating and even controlling patriarchal conditions. When Esperanza and her friends notice the rounding of their hips, they practise wiggling them because, as Esperanza knowledgeably tells her friends, 'You gotta be able to know what to do with hips when you get them' (p. 50). Unlike some of the women in the stories, Esperanza realises the power of her sexuality and the importance of learning to control it. The 'la Malinche' figure in the narrative is Esperanza's friend Sally, whose father says of her that to be 'this beautiful is trouble' (p. 81). Sally's sexual behaviour with the local boys is described by Esperanza as a betrayal in la Malinche-fashion: 'Sally had her own game' (p. 96). But unlike la Malinche, Cisneros implicitly suggests that Sally's actions were a response to her father's abuse of her, and her mother's neglect, thus figuring Sally's promiscuous behaviour as contingent upon circumstances beyond her control and thereby symbolically disrupting the *virgen/puta* dichotomy. Similarly, the 'Guadalupe' figure in the narrative is 'Aunt Lupe', Esperanza's sick aunt, who, while wasting away on her death bed, offers Esperanza encouragement and support by listening to and commenting upon the young girl's poems. Like la Virgen, she is long-suffering and self-sacrificing, but as with la Malinche, Cisneros connects Aunt Lupe's suffering with the harsh life of the barrio family, 'the kids who wanted to be kids instead of washing dishes and ironing their papa's shirts, and the husband who wanted a wife again' (p. 61).

The *virgen/puta* dichotomy is not the only symbolic opposition in the novel. Of equal significance is the emphasis placed upon the difference between a house and a home. The witch-woman in the text says to Esperanza: 'I see a home in the heart . . . A new house, a house made of heart' (p. 64). If Esperanza's name symbolises 'hope', then her overriding hope is for a home. 'Home' is not just a dwelling place, but also carries nuances of belonging, nurturance and origins. 'Home', as Kathleen Kirby puts it, is 'a walled site of belonging' (*Indifferent Boundaries: Spatial Concepts of Human Subjectivity*, Guildford Press, 1996, p. 21). More than a three-dimensional structure; it is a 'densely signifying marker in ideology' (Kirby, p. 21). 'Home' carries a heavy ideological weight. The yearning to belong is often linked to a desire for home ownership. As Marilyn Chandler makes clear in *Dwelling in the Text: Houses In American Fiction* (University of California Press, 1991), social and psychological stability is partly engendered through economic security and thus the goal of home ownership, one aspect of the American dream, is a preoccupation in much ethnic fiction. Chandler explores the predominance of houses as a cultural preoccupation in America: 'Our literature reiterates with remarkable consistency the centrality of the house in American cultural life and imagination' (p. 1). Chandler argues that, stemming from its position as a post-colonial country itself, America's cultural production has focused upon the necessity of carving out and claiming territory: 'In a country whose history has been focused for so long on the question of settlement and "development", the issue of how to stake out territory, clear it, cultivate it, and build on it has been of major economic, political and psychological consequence' (p. 1). Thus, part of the process of ethnic American self-definition has always been the definition of its space. And dominant nation-making ideologies have apprised the goal of home ownership: 'The American dream still expresses itself in the hope of owning a freestanding single-family dwelling, which to many remains the most significant measure of . . . cultural enfranchisement' (p. 1). For many ethnic writers in a state of 'unbelonging', the objective of home ownership especially signifies the move towards belonging to, as well as owning a corner in the world. This is something that Esperanza recognises early on. The narrative opens thus:

> We didn't always live on Mango Street. . . . The house on Mango Street is ours, and we don't have to pay rent to anybody, or share the yard with the people downstairs, or be careful not to make too much noise, and there isn't a landlord banging on the ceiling with a broom. But even so, it's not the house we thought we'd get. (p. 3)

Esperanza's assessment of their living quarters is carefully calculated and couched in precise economic terms. She recognises that economic stability leads to freedom: owning your own house means not having to answer to a landlord. Yet by the same logic, she is also aware that the house on Mango Street does not represent the fullest of possibilities:

> I knew then I had to have a house. A real house. One I could point to. But this isn't it. The house on Mango Street isn't it. For the time being, Mama says. Temporary, says Papa. But I know how those things go. (p. 5)

If the idea of a home represents freedom for Esperanza, then she is equally aware that the house can be a confining space for women. The house, as the realm of patriarchal control, can become a more hazardous place for women than the barrio outside: women are often depicted as locked in (like the woman Rafaela), abused (like Esperanza's friend Sally), or confined by domesticity (like Esperanza's mother). Learning this too, Esperanza's dream home becomes a female-only space. In the penultimate section, 'A House of My Own', Esperanza declares:

Not a flat. Not an apartment in back. Not a man's house. A house all my own. With my porch and my pillow, my pretty purple petunias. My books and my stories. My two shoes waiting beside the bed. Nobody to shake a stick at. Nobody's garbage to pick up after. Only a house quiet as snow, a space for myself to go, clean as paper before the poem. (p. 108)

This is Esperanza's version of Virginia Woolf's room of her own; a space devoid of female dependency, abuse, shame and noise. Sandra Cisneros dedicated *The House on Mango Street* 'A Las Mujeres/To the Women'. Her text not only gives Esperanza Cordero a home, it also carves a space for Chicana women in the house of fiction. Many commentators have observed the dominance of male writing in Chicano letters until relatively recently. Cisneros has said: 'the house in essence becomes you. You are the house' ('Solitary Fate', p. 73). Besides the echo of this quotation in the text, when the character Alicia tells Esperanza 'Like it or not you are Mango Street' (p. 107), Cisneros recognises in this statement the importance for Chicana writers of constructing a narrative tradition of their own, one which challenges masculinist Chicano assumptions and traditions.

Annotated Short Bibliography

Eysturoy, Annie O., *Daughters of Self-Creation: The Contemporary Chicana Novel* (University of New Mexico Press, 1996). With a focus on Chicana coming-of-age novels, where the adolescent protagonist is searching for her self-identity and her place in the world, Eysturoy's contention is that growing up Chicana involves the negotiation not only of gender issues but also those of race and class.

Gish, Robert Franklin, *Beyond Bounds: Cross-Cultural Essays on Anglo-American, Indian, and Chicano Literature* (University of New Mexico Press, 1996). In considering Chicano/a cultural production alongside that of other groups, a particularly useful book not only for examining attitudes towards the Chicano/as but also for placing Chicano/a literature in a broader context. Interesting and accessible.

Madsen, Deborah L., *Understanding Chicana Literature* (University of South Carolina Press, forthcoming). Focusing on the work of six contemporary Chicana writers in particular, an accessible and informative critical overview of Chicana literature since the 1970s.

Quintana, Alvina E., *Home Girls: Chicana Literary Voices* (Temple University Press, 1996). Seeking to interpret Chicana literature from an interdisciplinary perspective, this study is constructed as a series of accessible chapters which draw upon anthropological, historical, feminist and literary sources to examine both why and how some of the major Chicana authors write.

Saldívar, Ramón, *Chicano Narrative: The Dialectics of Difference* (University of Wisconsin Press, 1990). Highly influential critical study, intention of which is to promote the understanding of Chicano/a literature not only as a response to the social and historical experiences of its authors but also within the wider context of what constitutes 'America'. Looks in detail at various genres and certain works by key Chicano/a authors.

BRIDGET KEVANE ON CISNEROS'S PORTRAIT OF A BARRIO

Esperanza's journey is deeply rooted in her observations about her barrio. They aid her in coming to terms with her identity. Esperanza's search for her identity and her coming-of-age is universal; most readers will be able to identify with the feelings that trouble Esperanza—feelings of not belonging, of being other, of "the shame of being poor, of being female, of being not-quite-good-enough," as Cisneros states in the introduction to the tenth-anniversary edition (1993). The answer to these feelings, according to Cisneros, is to recover, celebrate, and always remember one's roots. In this respect, *The House on Mango Street* not only records Esperanza's story, but that of her *barrio*. Cisneros gives voice to the historically silenced members of the community. Esperanza records, as a writer, her own personal journey toward transformation, but also that of her neighborhood, a neighborhood that represents the collective story of Latino neighborhoods across the United States. Esperanza seeks to discover and clarify her identity through the members of her community—Mexicans, Puerto Ricans, Central Americans, legal and illegal immigrants, native people of color. The depiction of the *barrio* contains the collective themes of poverty, racism, migration, and patriarchy, and the subsequent destruction that they create in the community. Cisneros paints portraits of different characters, almost all trapped victims of social or patriarchal restrictions. Women withdraw behind locked doors and windows, and young men and women struggle to find meaning and validation in their *barrio* and in the world outside their neighborhood.

Cathy in "Cathy Queen of Cats" introduces the reader and Esperanza to the people in the neighborhood. When Esperanza and her family move in, Cathy, whose family is moving out, reveals that her own family is moving because the neighborhood is going downhill; Latinos like Esperanza and other people of color are moving in. The "neighborhood is getting bad" (13), she states. The fact that the narrator and Cathy are so young allows for these kinds of conversations, in which ethnic and racial differences are discussed in a matter-of-fact manner. As Cathy and Esperanza talk, Cathy describes everyone in the neighborhood. The neighborhood contains danger: Joe, the baby-grabber; Benny and Blanca, the corner store owners; and Edna, "the lady who owns the building next to you." Cathy also gives Esperanza advice about whom to befriend and whom not to befriend. She tells Esperanza not to become friends with Lucy and Rachel, whom she describes as "Two girls raggedy as rats." She tells Esperanza to stay away from Alicia, who has become "stuck-up" because she is in college.

After Cathy introduces the neighborhood, we are presented with several different portraits of the female members of the community. "There Was an Old Woman She Had so Many Children She Didn't Know What to Do" is a play on the old Mother Goose rhyme, "There Was an Old Lady Who Lived in a Shoe." Although the Mother Goose story also speaks of poverty, it does so in a whimsical manner. In turn, Cisneros's story reels from the poverty and many children that form the life of Rosa Vargas, "who cries every day for the man who left without even leaving a dollar for bologna" (*Mango Street* 29). Rosa Vargas also cries every day because she has too many children, and she is too tired to take care of them. She has so many children that she cannot watch them, and her son Angel dies from flying out a window "like a sugar donut, just like a falling star, and exploded down to earth without even an 'Oh'" (*Mango Street* 30). Alicia, the character in "Alicia Who Sees Mice," is motherless and afraid of mice, and perhaps of her father, the story suggests. Although she attends the university, she still must wake up early to make tortillas for her father. Mamacita in "No Speak English" arrives in the United States after her husband struggled to save money to bring her over. Mamacita never learns English and remains inside the apartment pining for her homeland. In "Rafaela Who Drinks Coconut & Papaya Juice on Tuesdays," Rafaela is young and married but is weary and trapped. Sally, in the story of the same name, is too beautiful. Her father tells her that being beautiful is trouble and, being "very strict in his religion" (81), he hits her frequently so she doesn't turn out like his sisters who, when he remembers them, make him sad. Of all the female characters in the collection, Esperanza feels a special affinity toward Sally and imagines a new home for her. Esperanza sees a home for Sally where the windows "would swing open"; all the sky would come in, where she could love without censure (82–83). Finally, there is Minerva, who writes poems but who is already married with two kids and a husband who has left her and keeps leaving, and who abuses her as well. Esperanza observes the vicious cycle—Minerva letting her husband continue to return, but also the fact that "her daughters will go that way too" (*Mango Street* 84).

There are portraits of young boys in the *barrio* as well. "Meme Ortiz," whose real name is Juan, moves into Cathy's house and breaks both arms jumping off a tree. "Louie, His Cousin & His Other Cousin," is the story of a Puerto Rican family. Louie's cousin steals a big yellow Cadillac, gives the neighborhood children a ride in it, and is caught by the police and taken away. The story demonstrates the abrupt end to Louie's cousin, who will most likely be placed in one juvenile detention center after another. "Geraldo No Last Name" describes an immigrant *bracero* (farm worker) who arrives in the United States seeking employment in order to send money home to his family. Geraldo, as described by the narrator, is "just another *brazer* (also a farm worker; English slang for *bracero*) who didn't speak English. Just another wetback" (*Mango Street* 66). Cisneros, however, provides the reader with a background for Geraldo, who arrives in the United States as a young boy, seen as invisible and without a history of any importance by the dominant class. Geraldo travels north, like so many other immigrants from Mexico, Central America, and South America, to financially help his family by sending money home every week. However, after being hit by a car, he is virtually left to die in the hospital. His family will most likely never discover what happened to him. Cisneros highlights the hospital staff's callousness toward Geraldo, just as she did the nun's callousness toward Esperanza. The surgeon never comes, the intern is not interested in aiding Geraldo because he has no name and, therefore, he is not important. By recording this story, Cisneros attempts to give Geraldo a history and a story, so that he becomes memorable as a person. Cisneros shows the callousness of society toward an illegal immigrant, but she includes Geraldo's story to demonstrate that we might have it all wrong. Someone seen as just another *bracero*, an immigrant worker who does not deserve medical care and who is left to die alone, is actually a hard-working man who is hoping to help his family survive.

Throughout these stories, we witness the people who make up the *barrio*, the invisible immigrants and the legal residents who are segregated because of color, race, or economic status. Many of these *barrio* portraits reveal the prejudice and misunderstanding prevalent in North American attitudes toward Latino communities. Each one of these stories gives voice to these problems on an emotional level so that we can identify with the characters and their struggle to survive in a foreign and, oftentimes, hostile environment. The creation of the *barrio* characters pays tribute to Cisneros's roots. The *barrio* is Esperanza's place of origin and, thus, synonymous with the origins of her identity. Esperanza observes, in both subtle and not so subtle forms, patriarchal oppression, domestic abuse, sexism, intolerance, oppression, bigotry, and poverty. Her sense of self will be derived from these observations; she realizes that she can potentially become any of the women she observes. That she survives, like the four skinny trees outside her window, is tribute to her strength, the strength of a young girl who already knows she does not want to inherit a place by the window. The collective community that surrounds her functions as a chorus of voices. They present her with advice, and they show her the potential dangers facing a young Mexican American girl on the verge of womanhood. Esperanza would not have remembered and returned to her roots without the voices of the other members of her community.

DARLENE PAGÁN ON COMMON SYMBOLS IN *THE HOUSE ON MANGO STREET*

Sandra Cisneros' *The House on Mango Street* consists of a series of vignettes set in a Chicago suburb that poignantly, and often painfully, reveal the joys and difficulties for young girls approaching womanhood. From observation and experience heightened by her coming of age, the narrator, Esperanza, begins questioning the distinctive situation of girls and boys and how this is reflected in and elaborated by the actions and interactions of women and men in her neighborhood. Through Esperanza's eyes, Cisneros provides teachers with a wealth of material for discussion of gender roles and issues that are often inextricably connected to race, class, power, and violence; the social construction of sex; female empowerment; and the feminization of poverty.

Esperanza recognizes immediately, in "Boys and Girls," that boys and girls live in separate universes where communication, particularly name calling and humiliation, maintains that separateness. From experience, however, Esperanza begins to recognize how gender distinctions continue into adulthood, for young girls, in a guise that appears to be both the object of their dreams—marriage and family—and the source of their pain and domination. In "Hips," for example, Esperanza and her friends imagine the day they will have hips and learn to move them to attract men, to dance, and to rock children to sleep; but, in "Rafaela Who Drinks Coconut & Papaya Juice on Tuesdays," the girls are saddened by the fate of a young bride who arrives at womanhood only to be physically locked inside, isolated from family and friends, by a possessive husband.

The most important symbol in the novel is the titular house which represents young girls' dreams for their own happy homes but also the prison that many homes are, guarded first by domineering fathers, and second by domineering husbands. The house also indicates a gender trap fortified by the cycle of poverty from which women and children suffer in their economic dependence on men. And while there are young women who cast off the passive role relegated to them, they must endure resulting difficulties and costs. In "Alice Who Sees Mice," Alice's mother has died and it is the daughter who must assume the household chores and care of her father, but her role as both her father's primary caregiver and a university student proves exhausting. At the end of the story, the narrator lauds Alice for being a good girl, for studying, and for seeing the mice her powerful father insists do not exist. In a parallel to David and Goliath, the mice symbolize Alice's persistence as she attempts to escape her father's domination and control. At the same time, she must also deal with her real potential for failure as a young woman entirely responsible for full-time work in and out of the home, in addition to her responsibilities to herself at the university.

One threat to young girls that Cisneros does not shy away from is the reality of violence against women. Two stories specifically address this subject in vivid though not graphic terms: "Minerva Writes Poems" and "Sally." In the former, a young girl refuses to leave her husband, even though he beats her, because he is the father of her children. In the latter, the narrator is raped by a group of boys near a carnival. As if the violence alone were not difficult enough, we learn that one of the boys had whispered about his victim, the narrator, being Spanish, conveying racist as well as sexist domination. Teachers will want to prepare readers before pursuing these particular stories by sharing the subject matter beforehand and perhaps also by asking readers about their understanding of and ideas about violence in women's lives. Such a discussion will help teachers recognize what their students do and do not know about violence against women, how they might react to the fiction, and what their multiple cultural contexts of violence are. Equally important is that teachers not fear addressing the subject of racism, but also not reinscribe stereotypes of brutish, Mexican men and passive, Mexican females. Cisneros' short story, "Woman Hollering Creek," as companion to the novel, presents possibilities for a young married woman resisting a husband who treats her badly.

To help articulate issues of race, class, and gender, but also of language and identity formation vivified by the metaphoric and geographic U.S./Mexican border, teachers can utilize any number of resources in Chicano/a studies and literature. Rafael Pérez-Torres specifically cites Cisneros' use of irony and humor to elaborate the tensions and ironies of men expected to claim power and women expected to relinquish theirs (198–200). Pérez-Torres also addresses symbolism in Cisneros' earlier fiction, including mythical and legendary females to exemplify power, which finds parallels in *Mango Street*, though not equivalents. In another vein, Cisneros' wealth of symbols in general might be compared among her works and also with the work of other authors who use common cultural symbols. The house as a symbol of confinement and liberation, for example, can be found in writers from Virginia Woolf (*A Room of One's Own*) to James Joyce (*Araby*). The recurring portrait of women physically and psychically immobilized as they sit in their houses, looking out of windows, and of girls' and women's sense of self as represented by shoe-imagery might respectively encourage creative classroom exploration as well as interesting parallels to classical literary texts (i.e., *Jane Eyre*, "The Yellow Wallpaper") or to folktales and children's stories ("Old Mother Hubbard," "Snow White," "Cinderella," *The Wizard of Oz*).

Despite the occasionally difficult subject matter, the narratives in *The House on Mango Street* are carried primarily by brave women who fight and succeed, and who love and laugh with an abandon that can inspire. Esperanza's name translates as hope in English; it thus signifies young girls' hopes for womanhood, but expressly for womanhood that represents empowerment as opposed to oppressiveness. Ultimately, that hope for empowerment extends not solely to women but to humanity in general.

Works by Sandra Cisneros

Bad Boys, 1980.

The House on Mango Street, 1983.

"Los Tejanos: Testimony to the Silenced," 1984.

"An Interview with Ana Castillo," 1984.

"Bread, Dreams and Poetry: Luis Omar Salinas, the Man," 1984.

"Salvador Late or Early," 1986.

"Cactus Flowers: In Search of Tejana Feminist Poetry," 1986.

My Wicked Wicked Ways, 1987.

"Ghosts and Voices: Writing from Obsession," 1987.

"Notes to a Young(er) Writer," 1987.

"Do You Know Me? I Wrote The House on Mango Street," 1987.

Woman Hollering Creek and Other Stories, 1991.

Loose Woman: Poems, 1994.

"Guadalupe the Sex Goddess," 1996.

Hairs/Pelitos, 1997.

Caramelo, 2002.

Vintage Cisneros, 2004.

Annotated Bibliography

Augenbraum, Harold, and Margarite Fernández Olmos, eds. *U. S. Latino Literature: A Critical Study Guide for Students and Teachers.* Westport, Connecticut, and London: Greenwood Press, 2000.

Each essay deals with one writer and his or her work. One chapter is devoted to Cisneros and *The House on Mango Street.* Several appendices are also included with suggestions for approaches to teaching Latino/a literature in the classroom, a resource for gay and lesbian authors and their work, resources available on the World Wide Web, and suggestions for additional study.

Cruz, Felicia J. "On the Simplicity of Sandra Cisneros's *House on Mango Street.*" *Modern Fiction Studies* 47:4 (Winter 2001): pp. 910–45.

In this essay, Cruz suggests that the readings of *The House on Mango Street* have exaggerated the simplicity of the text. She contends that the text and its relative depth depend upon the cultural cache, agenda, education and experience of the reader. Much of her analysis uses Terry Eagleton's *Literary Theory: An Introduction* as a lens through which one might question the rhetoric of the book.

Daniels, Patsy J. *The Voice of the Oppressed in the Language of the Oppressor: A Discussion of Selected Postcolonial Literature from Ireland, Africa and America.* New York: Routledge, 2001.

In her introduction to this far-ranging book, Daniels links formerly marginalized writers like Yeats, Joyce, Conrad, and Achebe with minority ethnic women writers because the latter, as the former had once to do, are recovering and revising the past in such a way to fit themselves and describing the oppression they have endured attempting to bring legitimacy to their work. Daniels also points out that unlike their male predecessors, the women writers automatically belong to the most marginalized of margins because of their gender, and therefore, in their own writing, cannot and do not leave out of consideration any groups in the population. Students interested in the perspectives offered in this book should become familiar with the writings of the once-marginalized and now-canonical male writers Daniels discusses.

De Valdés, Maria Elena. "In Search of Identity in Cisneros's *The House on Mango Street.*" *Canadian Review of American Studies* 23:1 (Fall 1992): pp. 55–72.

De Valdés writes about the connection that must occur between the speaking protagonist and the protagonist in actuality. She argues that Esperanza must be her speech; it acts as a continuation and manifestation of the self, based on observation both within and without. She integrates into the argument recognition of the marginalization of the character based on her feminist inclinations and Chicana heritage.

Doyle, Jacqueline. "More Room of Her Own: Sandra Cisneros's *The House on Mango Street.*" MELUS 19:4 (1994): pp. 5–35.

In this article, Doyle explores the ways in which Cisneros complicates Virginia Woolf's notion of "a room of one's own." Doyle pays particular attention to the effect of ethnicity on this "feminist inheritance."

Eysturoy, Annie O. *Daughters of Self-Creation: The Contemporary Chicana Novel.* Albuquerque: University of New Mexico Press, 1996.

Like Deborah L. Madsen (see pp. 106–07), Annie O. Eysturoy concerns herself with issues of race and class as well as gender. Her study focuses on coming-of-age fiction where the protagonist is an adolescent female who must contend with race and class issues along with her efforts to create/discover her identity. One section of the author's discussion focuses on *The House on Mango Street.*

Fisher, Jerilyn, and Ellen S. Silber, eds. *Women in Literature: Reading through the Lens of Gender.* Westport, Connecticut, and London: Greenwood Press, 2003.

The editors of this volume have chosen 96 examples from world literature of novels, stories, and plays to examine the treatment of and attitude toward women over the centuries and throughout nations. Each writer and work of art is discussed briefly with a section on the works cited and suggestions for further reading. An appendix provides a thematic list of the books with topics such as "Young Girls and Adolescents," "Mothers and Daughters," "Women as Sex Objects," Women's Search for Freedom," "Men's Power over Women," and others dealing with roles, stereotypes, violence, and marriage. The book is a good beginner's introduction to world literature with a central theme as focus.

Ganz, Robin. "Sandra Cisneros: Border Crossings and Beyond." *MELUS* 19:1 (Spring 1994): pp. 19–29.

Ganz provides basic background information on the author, linking her autobiographical experiences to the creation of Esperanza and her world and world views in *The House on Mango Street*.

Grice, Helena, Candida Hepworth, Maria Lauret, and Martin Padget, eds. *Beginning Ethnic American Literatures*. Manchester and New York: Manchester University Press, 2001.

Each of the four editors takes on one area of ethnic American literature—Native American, African American, Asian American, and Chicano/a fiction. In the introduction, one of the editors, Maria Lauret, writes an impassioned piece about the urgent need for familiarity with ethnic literature and its life-saving meaning for many ethnic Americans. She also presents a thoughtful analysis of what the American national "identity" promised to be and what it actually is for many people. The editors include an extensive annotated bibliography to aid and encourage more attention to this subject.

Gutiérrez-Jones, Leslie S. "Different Voices: The Re-Building of the Barrio in Sandra Cisneros' *The House of Mango Street*." *Anxious Power: Reading, Writing, and Ambivalence in Narrative by Women*. Eds. Carol J. Singley and Susan Elizabeth

Sweeney. Albany: State University of New York Press, 1993: pp. 295–312.

In this essay, Gutiérrez-Jones discusses the way in which Cisneros manipulates the bildungsroman form to suit the needs of a female, bi-ethnic narrator and author. Because both the author and her protagonist need to find space and freedom outside the cultural constraints of the barrio and white patriarchal culture, they need to shift the form so as not to become trapped again in the language and traditions of the oppressor.

Herrera-Sobek, María. "The Politics of Rape: Sexual Transgression in Chicana Fiction." *Chicana Creativity and Criticism: New Frontiers in American Literature, 2nd Ed.* Eds. María Herrera-Sobek and Helena María Viramontes. Albuquerque: University of New Mexico Press, 1996: pp. 245–56.

Herrera-Sobek examines rape as a metaphor in the work of Chicana writers, emphasizing that the metaphor is doubly powerful coming from the perspective of the twice marginalized Chicano female. The lens through which it is viewed is feminist which reinforces the idea that rape becomes the physical manifestation of patriarchal or phallocentric society. She posits that the metaphor is used to reject the oppression of women on multiple levels, from the broadest societal norms to the familial and individual. She asserts that the difference between Chicana fiction and that of other feminist writers utilizing the metaphor stems from the communal context in which the Chicana writers place the incidents.

Horno-Delago, Asunción, Eliana Ortega, Nina M. Scott, and Nancy Saporta Sternbach, eds. *Breaking Boundaries: Latina Writing and Critical Readings.* Amherst: The University of Massachusetts Press, 1989.

The editors met at a 1986 symposium on Spanish and Portuguese Bilingualism and decided to make a collective effort to bring Latina writing away from its often-marginal position into greater public light. They assert that the bilingual and "interlingual" features of Latina literature—largely responsible for its exclusion from traditional literary studies—are improperly under-appreciated because historically it was the Chicana communities that established the first literary heritage in the United States. They quote Luis Valdez: "We did not, in fact, come to the United States at all. The United States came to us" (xii). The authors make no attempt to interfere with or comment on the ideological categories of their contributors or the writers themselves and they intend the work to legitimize a space for Latina writing in academic and publishing centers.

Kevane, Bridget. *Latino Literature in America*. Westport, Connecticut, and London: Greenwood Press, 2003.

In her introduction, Kevane reminds her readers of the importance of literature for becoming—relatively effortlessly—informed about the social, cultural and political record of people very different from themselves. She is further interested in delineating important differences within the Latino communities and mentions specifically Latinos, Chicanos, Nuevo Mexicanos, Cubanos, Nuyoricans, Puerto Ricans, Boricuas, Dominicanos, Quisqueyanos, and Mexican Americanos. Her essay on Sandra Cisneros discusses both *The House on Mango Street* and *Woman Hollering Creek*. Other writers discussed are: Julia Alvarez, Rudolfo Anaya, Junot Díaz, Cristina García, Oscar Hijuelos, Judith Ortiz Cofer, and Ernesto Quinonez. Substantial familiarity with the subject is required for this study.

Kevane, Bridget, and Juanita Heredia, eds. *Latina Self-Portraits: Interviews with Contemporary Women Writers*. Albuquerque: University of New Mexico Press, 2000.

Like other books in this list, this study focuses on women writers. Ten established Latina writers are interviewed about their cultural roots, heritage, upbringing, and other more personal issues that have not been looked at for academic purposes. The editors undertake this project believing that Latina literature has been coming into its own for the three decades that precede the book's publication. The editors also discuss critically the disparaging remarks often made about

Latino literature—an example being Cisneros' *The House on Mango Street* for its use of "simple" language. Other writers discussed are Julia Alvarez, Denise Chávez, Rosario Ferré, Cristina García, Nicholasa Mohr, Cherríe Moraga, Judith Ortiz Cofer, Esmeralda Santiago, and Helena María Viramontes.

Kuribayashi, Tomoko. "The Chicana Girl Writes Her Way In and Out: Space and Bilingualism in Sandra Cisneros' *The House on Mango Street*." *Creating Safe Spaces: Violence and Women's Writings.* Eds. Tomoko Kuribayashi and Julie Tharpe. Albany: State University of New York Press, 1998, 165–77.

In this article, Kuribayashi places the protagonist, Esperanza, in three categories of marginalization: She is biethnic, female, and poverty stricken. Because of these identities, Esperanza is forced to find new spaces to inhabit as the patriarchal culture from which she springs keeps her from having power as a woman, the house that she inhabits keeps her from having the social power of the signified wealthy, and her ethnic identity will prohibit her from mainstreaming into white middle America. She overcomes these problems by integrating her identities, using the spaces between English and Spanish to create a Utopian vision wherein she can acquire wealth but use it to better the lives of the people in the barrio, particularly the disenfranchised like the women around her and the homeless.

Madsen, Deborah L. *Understanding Contemporary Chicana Literature.* Columbia: University of South Carolina Press, 2000.

Madsen begins her commentaries on six Chicana writers with an introduction outlining the main features of this literary movement that began after the civil rights struggles of the sixties. Informed by specifically feminist and political experiences of that decade, Madsen is interested in delineating the differences in approach to hierarchies of power by white feminists and women of color. She points out that access by white women to positions of power in the male-dominated culture—using the tools of affirmative action and equal opportunity programs—has not changed the hierarchies of power or helped establish a more just society for al citizens. Sandra Cisneros is among the six Chicana writers discussed, and all the critical analysis throughout the book focuses on how the women address these larger issues.

Matchie, Thomas. "Literary Continuity in Sandra Cisneros's *The House on Mango Street.*" *The Midwest Quarterly* 37:1 (Autumn 1995): pp. 67–79.

Matchie suggests that Cisneros' *The House on Mango Street* fits as the third novel in Edgar Branch's notion of "literary continuity" which begins with Mark Twain's *The Adventures of Huckleberry Finn* and Salinger's *The Catcher in the Rye*. Like her predecessors, Cisneros writes a coming of age novel of a young protagonist profoundly affected by cultural norms. In terms of linguistic technique and use of archetype, Matchie suggests that this novel, though it is told by a young Chicano female, still fits into this American literary tradition.

McCracken, Ellen. "Sandra Cisneros' *The House on Mango Street*: Community-Oriented Introspection and the Demystification of Patriarchal Violence." *Breaking Boundaries: Latina Writing and Critical Readings*. Eds. Asunción Horno-Delgado, Eliana Ortega, Nina M. Scott, and Nancy Saporta Sternbach. Amherst: The University of Massachusetts Press, 1989: pp. 62–71.

McCracken discusses the way in which Cisneros complicates the traditional male-oriented vision of the Bildungsroman in multiple ways, first giving a female perspective, second giving it a Chicana communal perspective, and third redefining its linguistic and ideological traditions. McCracken gives particular emphasis to the question of whether the book will be able to make its way into the literary canon without the current vogue of the highly individualistic search for self that defines those texts of the same genre. She questions whether the academy will embrace the idea of a communal creation of self, with particular attention paid to the collective creation of female identity within community spaces.

Norton, Jody. "History, Rememory, Transformation: Actualizing Literary Value." *The Centennial Review* 38:3 (Fall 1994): pp. 589–602.

In this article, Norton examines the idea John Ellis espouses: "[T]exts are made into literature by the community, not by the authors." Norton examines the way in which readers interact with and engage Esperanza and the literary text as an act of mutual identity formation.

Olivares, Julián. "Sandra Cisneros' *House on Mango Street* and the Poetics of Space." *Chicana Creativity and Criticism: New Frontiers in American Literature, 2nd Ed.* Eds. María Herrera-Sobek and Helena María Viramontes. Albuquerque: University of New Mexico Press, 1996: pp. 233–44.

Olivares explores the notion of space and the way in which Cisneros plays with Gaston Bachelard's idea of *The Poetics of Space*. Cisneros also treats the metaphor of poetics of space but in so doing she revisions one of its primary tenants, "the dialectic of the inside and outside" changing the inside from a place of inclusion to a space of subjugation particularly for Chicana women.

Petty, Leslie. "The 'Dual'-ing images of la Malinche and la Virgen de Guadalupe in Cisneros's *The House on Mango Street*." *MELUS* 25:2 (Summer 2000): pp. 119–32.

Petty examines the effect of two archetypal female representations, la Malinche and la Virgen de Guadalupe, in Cisneros's *The House on Mango Street*. She discusses the cultural importance of the Virgin and the Whore to the Mexican culture and the way in which it manifests itself in the novel.

Poey, Delia. "Coming of Age in the Curriculum: *The House on Mango Street* and *Bless Me, Ultima* as Representative Texts." *The Americas Review* 24:3/4 (Fall/Winter 1996): pp. 201–17.

Poey attempts to answer some of the culture war questions raised by E.D. Hirsch and Allan Bloom in the 1980s regarding multiculturalism in the educational system. She seeks to define what is meant by multiculturalism and to show the ways in which these texts interact with the established traditions of the canon and the communities they seek to represent.

Quintana, Alvina E. *Home Girls: Chicana Literary Voices.* Philadelphia: Temple University Press, 1996.

The author introduces the work with a discussion of her formative years in which she was unaware of living a "bi-cultural" life. Later, she was impelled to notice and analyze the phenomenon of "hybrid" lifestyles. She points out that Chicana literature has its origins in cross-disciplinary categories. To her understanding of Chicana literature, Quintana brings perspectives from anthropology, feminism, history, and literature. She is interested in how Latina writers actually craft their work. One of the five chapters focuses on *The House on Mango Street.*

Saldívar, Ramón. *Chicano Narrative: The Dialectics of Difference.* Madison: The University of Wisconsin Press, 1990.

This seminal work on Chicano literature requires some formal understanding of literary theory and the standards for acceptance in the traditional canons. Saldívar makes much of his argument using the insights of structuralism, poststructuralism, deconstruction, and feminist and Marxist theories. He questions whether using these methods and insights can be used to legitimize literary works from outside the dominant culture. Saldívar intends to demonstrate that Chicano/a literature can be understood not only as being in resistance to traditional American literature but as being essential to an expanded idea of what American literature is and has accomplished.

Scalise Sugiyama, Michelle. "Of Woman Bondage: The Eroticism of Feet in *The House on Mango Street.*" *The Midwest Quarterly* 41:1 (Autumn 1999): pp. 9–20.

Scalise Sugiyama explores the eroticism of feet and shoes as a metaphor for men's exertion of control over women. She cites multiple ways in which the feet and their adornment reinforce the patriarchal power structure and traces that theme throughout the book as a larger metaphor.

Sommers, Joseph, and Tomás Ybarra-Frausto, eds. *Modern Chicano Writers: A Collection of Critical Essays*. New York: Prentice-Hall, Inc., 1979.

Of the two editors, Joseph Sommers writes from direct experiences with Mexican Americans working both legally and illegally in the United States. In their introduction to the volume, they cite the year 1848 as the beginning of Chicano literature—when the United States annexed portions of Mexico, which compelled thousands of Mexicans to become American citizens. The editors also point out that Chicano literature was created out of a need for cultural expression by peoples judged to be marginal. As such, it serves survivalist purposes, both personal and collective.

Szadziuk, Maria. "Culture as Transition: Becoming a Woman in Bi-Ethnic Space." *Mosaic* 32:3 (September 1999): pp. 109–29.

Szadziuk explores, via three Chicano writers, the notion of "culture-in-transition" and the way in which each of the authors treats the idea within their autobiographical works. She asks specifically what the effect of distance from the dominant culture (first/second/third generation) has had on the narrative techniques and modes of the texts in question.

Tatum, Charles M. *Chicano and Chicana Literature*. Tucson: University of Arizona Press, 2006.

Although the author is attempting a comprehensive treatment of the origins, developments, current status and participants in the expanding world of Chicano/a literature, he writes in such clear and concise prose his book is appropriate for both advanced students and those just becoming acquainted with the subject. Poetry, theater, autobiography, novels, and short stories are covered along with a brief discussion of each artist. The book has an extensive bibliography and includes 36 photographs of the different writers he is discussing.

Yarbro-Bejarano, Yvonne. "Chicana Literature from a Chicana Feminist Perspective." *Chicana Creativity and Criticism: New Frontiers in American Literature, 2nd Ed.* Eds. María

Herrera-Sobek and Helena María Viramontes. Albuquerque: University of New Mexico Press, 1996. pp. 213–19.

In this essay, Yarbro-Bejarano explains the distinct nature of the Chicana Feminist perspective as it differs from that of white Feminism and the Chicana perspective. She emphasizes the idea that Chicana feminism is born of the neighborhoods, barrios, and streets within which these women live and work. As a result, the search for self in this type of literature necessarily recognizes the community and its part of freeing/enslaving the self. This point of view also critically integrates communal history in the United States, paying particular attention to racism and sexism within the community as well as without. She utilizes the works of particular Chicana writers to establish both the history of the perspective and its manifestations in the literature.

 Contributors

Harold Bloom is Sterling Professor of the Humanities at Yale University. Educated at Cornell and Yale universities, he is the author of more than 30 books, including *Shelley's Mythmaking* (1959), *The Visionary Company* (1961), *Blake's Apocalypse* (1963), *Yeats* (1970), *The Anxiety of Influence* (1973), *A Map of Misreading* (1975), *Kabbalah and Criticism* (1975), *Agon: Toward a Theory of Revisionism* (1982), *The American Religion* (1992), *The Western Canon* (1994), *Omens of Millennium: The Gnosis of Angels, Dreams, and Resurrection* (1996), *Shakespeare: The Invention of the Human* (1998), *How to Read and Why* (2000), *Genius: A Mosaic of One Hundred Exemplary Creative Minds* (2002), *Hamlet: Poem Unlimited* (2003), *Where Shall Wisdom Be Found?* (2004), and *Jesus and Yahweh: The Names Divine* (2005). In addition, he is the author of hundreds of articles, reviews, and editorial introductions. In 1999, Professor Bloom received the American Academy of Arts and Letters' Gold Medal for Criticism. He has also received the International Prize of Catalonia, the Alfonso Reyes Prize of Mexico, and the Hans Christian Andersen Bicentennial Prize of Denmark.

Joseph Sommers was, at the time of his essay, professor of Latin American literature at the University of California at San Diego. He has worked on border issues and the plight of the undocumented worker. His published works include *After the Storm: Landmarks of the Modern Mexican Novel* and (co-author) *Chicano Literature: Text and Context* (1972).

Ellen McCracken has written widely on Latin American culture, history, and literature. She teaches contemporary Latin American literature and cultural studies in the department of Spanish and Portuguese at the University of California at Santa Barbara. Published works include *From Mademoiselle to Ms: Decoding Women's Magazines* (1993) and *New Latina Narrative: The Feminine Space of Postmodern Ethnicity* (1979).

Annie O. Eysturoy has taught American literature in the United States and Spain; she is currently teaching in the Faroe Islands.

Myrna-Yamil Gonzáles was, at the time of publication, adjunct professor at Brooklyn College. She has published frequently in *Culturadoor*.

Deborah L. Madsen teaches American literature at the University of Geneva. A prolific author, she has also published *Post-Colonial Literature* (1999), *Feminist Theory and Literary Practice* (2000), and edited *Disaporic Histories: Cultural Archives of Chinese Transnationalism* (2009).

Patsy J. Daniels is assistant professor of English at Jackson State University in Jackson, Mississippi. She is also the author of *The Voice of the Oppressed*.

Helena Grice teaches in the department of English and creative writing at the University of Aberystwyth in Wales.

Bridget Kevane is professor of Spanish in the department of modern languages and literatures and professor of Latin American and Latino literature at Montana State University in Bozeman, Montana. She is also chairwoman of the department of modern languages and literatures.

Darlene Pagán is assistant professor of ethnic literature and creative writing at Pacific University in Forest Grove, Oregon. Her poetry has been published in *The MacGuffin*, *Evansville Review*, and *West Wind Review*.

Acknowledgments

Index

Characters are indexed by first name (e.g., Esperanza Cordero).